Ami Pro
Made Simple

Made Simple *Computer Books*

- **easy to follow**
- **jargon free**
- **practical**
- **task based**
- **easy steps**

All you want are the **basics**, you don't want to be bothered with all the advanced stuff, or be engulfed in technical mumbo jumbo. You have neither the time nor the interest in knowing about every feature, function or command and you don't want to wade through big computer books on the subject or stumble through the maze of information in the manuals. The

MADE SIMPLE series is **for you**!

You want to **learn quickly what's essential** and **how** to do things with a particular piece of software... you're:

- **a Secretary**, or **temp** for example...who wants to **get the job done**, **quickly** and **efficiently**

- **a Manager**, without the time to learn all about the software but who wants to **produce   letters, memos, reports, spreadsheets**

- someone **working from home** using the software, who needs a **self teaching**

  approach, that gives **results fast**, with the least confusion.

By a combination of **tutorial approach**, with **tasks to do**, and **easy steps** the **MADE SIMPLE** series of Computer Books stands above all others.

See the complete series at your **local bookstore now**, or in case of difficulty, contact Reed Book Services Ltd., Orders Dept, PO Box 5, Rushden, Northants, NN10 9YX. Tel 0933 58521. Fax 0933 50284. Credit card sales 0933 410511.

Series titles:

AmiPro	Moira Stephen	0 7506 2067 6
Excel	Stephen Morris	0 7506 2070 6
Lotus 123	Ian Robertson	0 7506 2066 8
MS-Dos	Ian Sinclair	0 7506 2069 2
MS-Works	P. K. McBride	0 7506 2065 X
Windows	P. K. McBride	0 7506 2072 2
Word	Keith Brindley	0 7506 2071 4
WordPerfect	Stephen Copestake	0 7506 2068 4

Ami Pro
Made Simple

Moira Stephen

Made Simple
BOOKS

Made Simple
An imprint of Butterworth-Heinemann Ltd
Linacre House, Jordan Hill, Oxford OX2 8DP

Ⓡ A member of the Reed Elsevier plc group

OXFORD   LONDON   BOSTON
MUNICH   NEW DELHI   SINGAPORE   SYDNEY
TOKYO   TORONTO   WELLINGTON

First published 1994
© Moira Stephen 1994

TRADEMARKS/REGISTERED TRADEMARKS
Computer hardware and software brand names mentioned in this book are
protected by their respective trademarks and are acknowledged.

British Library Cataloguing in Publication Data
A catalogue record for this book is available from the British Library

ISBN 0 7506 2067 6

🐫 Typeset by P.K.McBride, Southampton
Set in Archetype, Cotswold Book and Gravity from Advanced Graphics Ltd.
Icons designed by Sarah Ward © 1994
Printed and bound in Great Britain
by Scotprint, Musselburgh, Scotland

Contents

Preface

The computer is about as simple as a spacecraft, and who ever let an untrained spaceman loose? You pick up a manual that weighs more than your birth-weight, open it and find that its written in computerspeak. You see messages on the screen that look like code and the thing even makes noises. No wonder that you feel it's your lucky day if everything goes right. What do you do if everything goes wrong? Give up.

Training helps. Being able to type helps. Experience helps. This book helps, by providing training and assisting with experience. It can't help you if you always manage to hit the wrong keys, but it can tell you which are the right ones and what to do when you hit the wrong ones. After some time, even the dreaded manual will start to make sense, just because you know what the writers are wittering on about.

Computing is not black magic. You don't need luck or charms, just a bit of understanding. The problem is that the programs that are used nowadays look simple but aren't. Most of them are crammed with features you don't need – but how do you know what you don't need? This book shows you what is essential and guides you through it. You will know how to make an action work and why. The less essential bits can wait – and once you start to use a program with confidence you can tackle these bits for yourself.

The writers of this series have all been through it. We know your time is valuable, and you don't want to waste it. You don't buy books on computer subjects to read jokes or be told that you are a dummy. You want to find what you need and be shown how to achieve it. Here, at last, you can.

1 In and out of Ami Pro

Getting into Ami Pro

Getting into Ami Pro is like getting into any other Windows application. If Windows is not running, you must go into Windows and display the Program Manager Window.

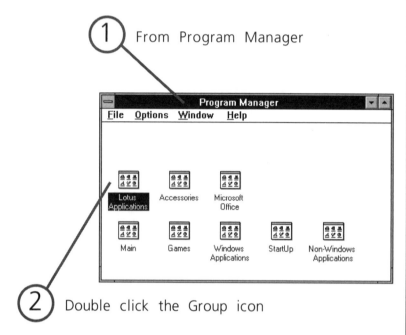

From Program Manager

Double click the Group icon

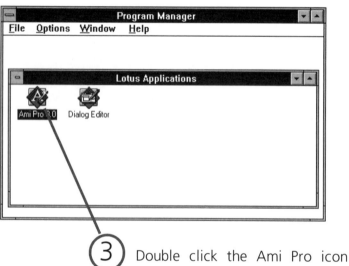

Double click the Ami Pro icon

1 Display the Program Manager Window

2 Open the group that has Ami Pro in it (Ami Pro may be in a different group on your machine - it depends on how it has been set up)

3 Open the application by double clicking the Ami Pro icon

❑ The Ami Pro copyright screen appears, then the Ami Pro work screen, and you are ready to start typing.

Take note

It is assumed that **Ami Pro** is installed on your machine.

2

The Ami Pro screen

Once into Ami Pro, you are ready to start work. A new document is open ready for you to key in your text. You do not need to do anything, but type!

You are probably familiar with the basic elements in a window, but here is a guide to the Ami Pro screen so you know what's what!

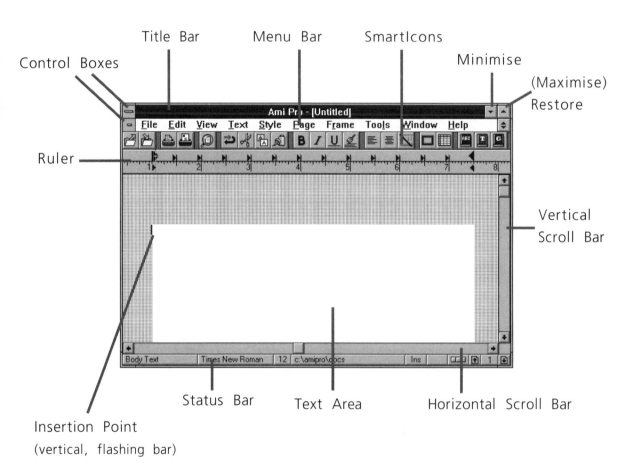

Title Bar   Menu Bar   SmartIcons

Control Boxes

Minimise

(Maximise) Restore

Ruler

Vertical Scroll Bar

Status Bar   Text Area   Horizontal Scroll Bar

Insertion Point (vertical, flashing bar)

Exiting Ami Pro

When you have finished your session in Ami Pro you must close the application down and return to the Windows environment. Any documents you have been working on should be saved if necessary. If you forget to save a document, Ami Pro will prompt you before it closes down.

Basic steps

1 Double click the *top* **Control Box** on the Title Bar

or

Choose **Exit** from the **File** menu

Ami Pro - [Untitled]

File   Edit   View   Text   Style   Page   Frame   Tools   Window   Help

Body Text   Times New Roman   12   c:\amipro\docs   Ins

① Double click

① Open the File menu

choose Exit

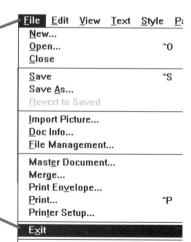

File   Edit   View   Text   Style   P:

New...
Open...   ^O
Close

Save   ^S
Save As...
Revert to Saved

Import Picture...
Doc Info...
File Management...

Master Document...
Merge...
Print Envelope...
Print...   ^P
Printer Setup...

Exit

1 GSDOC1.SAM

4

2 If you have not saved your file, or if you have made changes since you last saved your file, a prompt appears on the screen. Respond as appropriate.

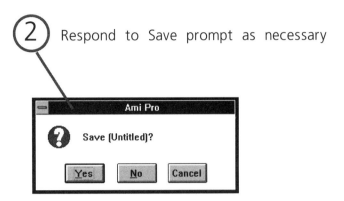

Respond to Save prompt as necessary

Save options

Yes

Saves the document before exiting Ami Pro. If the document has *never* been saved, this option takes you to the **Save As** dialog box so you can give your file a name.

(See SAVE in next section)

No

Exits Ami Pro without saving the document

Cancel

Returns you to the document so you can continue work

Summary

❏ To access Ami Pro, double click the Group icon that Ami Pro is in, then double click the Application icon.

❏ You can start typing as soon as you are into Ami Pro - a new document is open for you.

❏ Exit Ami Pro either by choosing **Exit** from the **File** Menu, or by double clicking the control box on the Title Bar.

2   Basic file handling

Creating a new file

When you go into Ami Pro initially, a new document is already open for you so you can start work straight away. However, as you complete one task and progress to another, you will need to open a new file for each document you intend to work on.

It is **not** advisable to put all your work in one file. If you mix your reports, letters and memos up in one file, you eventually end up with a BIG file, and to find a particular report or letter, you would have to scroll through the file until you found it. Also, should you accidentally delete the file, you have lost the lot!!

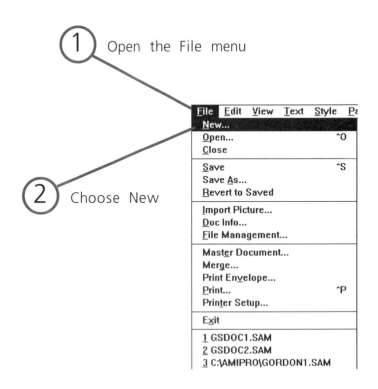

1 Open the **File** Menu

2 Choose **New...**

3 At the **New File** dialog box, choose the **Style Sheet** you want to base your document on. The one suggested, the *Default*, is the one you want to use.

4 Modify the options as required. If the check box beside an option has a cross in it, it is selected, if there is no cross, it isn't. If you click on a box, the cross is switched on or off. The default options are fine, so you don't need to change anything.

5 Click on the **OK** button to create a new document based on the selected style sheet.

Options

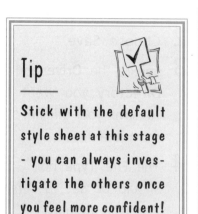

With Contents

If the Style sheet contains text or graphics, they will be included in your new document if you select this check box.

Run Macro

If the Style sheet has been set up with macros to run when it is used, they will run if this check box is selected

List by description

If selected, a description of the Style sheet is displayed, and the name of the file appears at the bottom of the dialog box. If not selected, the name of the Style sheet is displayed and the description appears at the bottom.

Close current file

If selected, the current file will be closed when the new file is created. If the box is clear, you can create a new file and keep your existing file open.

Preview

If selected, a preview of the Style sheet is displayed to the right of the dialog box.

(5) Click OK

(3) Select Style Sheet

(4) Modify options if necessary

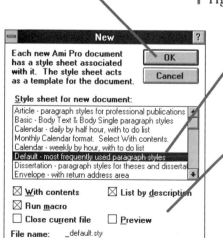

New

Each new Ami Pro document has a style sheet associated with it. The style sheet acts as a template for the document.

OK

Cancel

Style sheet for new document:

Article - paragraph styles for professional publications
Basic - Body Text & Body Single paragraph styles
Calendar - daily by half hour, with to do list
Monthly Calendar format. Select With contents.
Calendar - weekly by hour, with to do list
Default - most frequently used paragraph styles
Dissertation - paragraph styles for theses and dissertat
Envelope - with return address area

☒ With contents   ☒ List by description
☒ Run macro
☐ Close current file   ☐ Preview
File name: _default.sty

Saving a file

Once you have created a document you must Save it. If you don't save it, it will be lost when you come out of Ami Pro and you will need to re-type it again should you need it.

If you are working on a long document it is a good idea to save it regularly and not wait until you have completed the whole thing.

If there is a power cut, or your computer crashes for some reason, documents not saved are lost and you have to type them in again!

Basic steps

1 Open the **File** Menu

2 Choose **Save**.

3 Select the **Drive** and **Directory** you want to save your file in, from the lists

4 The **File Type** box should be set to *Ami Pro* (the default)

5 Give your file a **Name** (maximum of 8 characters, no spaces or punctuation allowed)

6 Type in a **description** for your document if required

7 Click the **OK** button

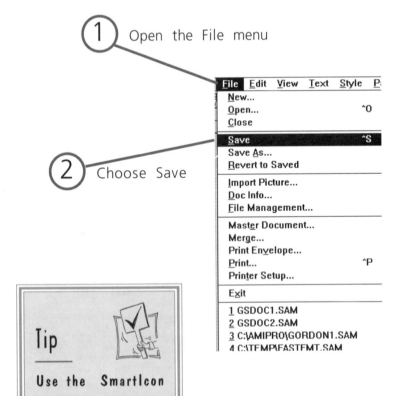

(1) Open the File menu

(2) Choose Save

File   Edit   View   Text   Style   P:
New...
Open...   ^o
Close

Save   ^S
Save As...
Revert to Saved

Import Picture...
Doc Info...
File Management...

Master Document...
Merge...
Print Envelope...
Print...   ^P
Printer Setup...

Exit

1 GSDOC1.SAM
2 GSDOC2.SAM
3 C:\AMIPRO\GORDON1.SAM
4 C:\TEMP\FASTFMT.SAM

Tip

Use the SmartIcon or [Ctrl]-[S] as a shortcut to the Save dialog box.

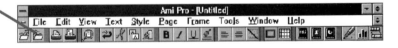

DIRECTORY CAN ONLY BE SELECTED IN DRIVE C

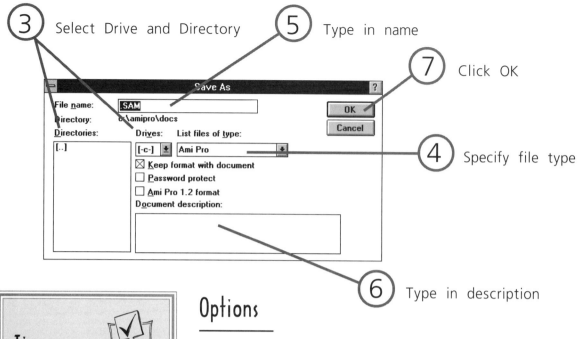

③ Select Drive and Directory   ⑤ Type in name

⑦ Click OK

④ Specify file type

⑥ Type in description

Options

Keep format with document

Keep this selected, then every time you access your document it will be formatted as you intended

Password Protect

If you want your document to have a password, select this option. But beware!! - don't forget the password as you will be asked for it when you next open the document.

Ami Pro 1.2 format

If you want to save your document in this format, select this option.

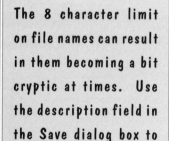

Tip

The 8 character limit on file names can result in them becoming a bit cryptic at times. Use the description field in the Save dialog box to give an explanation of the file's contents.

Take note

Once you have saved your file, you can quickly re-save it any time you edit it simply by clicking the SmartIcon or [Ctrl]-[S]. The edited file replaces the original file.

Auto timed save

You can get Ami Pro to save your document automatically after a specified time has elapsed (you can specify a range between 1 and 99 minutes).

You have to save your document using the **Save** (or **Save As**) command as usual, stipulating the drive, directory and file name. If you edit your document, with the **Auto Timed Save** function selected, your document will be re-saved automatically as specified.

This is a very useful option when working on long documents where you want to save regularly rather then wait until the document is complete, or when you are doing a lot of editing, and want to save the changes regularly.

Basic steps

1 Open the **Tools** menu

2 Choose **User Setup**

3 Select the **Auto timed save** option

4 Specify the time required between Auto Saves for your documents (between 1 and 99 minutes)

5 Click **OK**

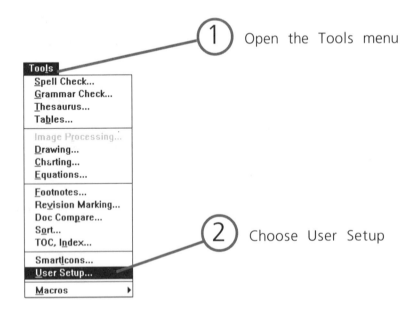

① Open the Tools menu

Tools

Spell Check...
Grammar Check...
Thesaurus...
Ta**b**les...
Image Processing...
Drawing...
Charting...
Equations...
Footnotes...
Re**v**ision Marking...
Doc Com**p**are...
S**o**rt...
TOC, I**n**dex...
Smart**I**cons...
User Setup...
Macros ▶

② Choose User Setup

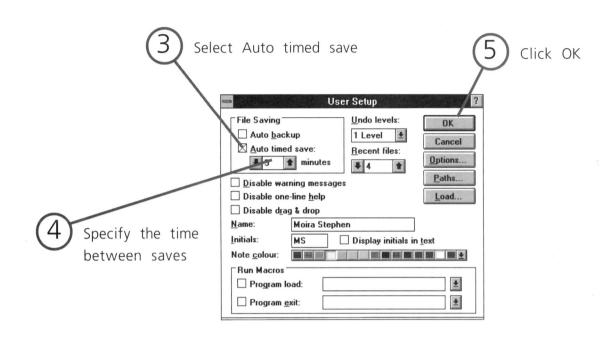

③ Select Auto timed save

⑤ Click OK

④ Specify the time between saves

Auto Backup

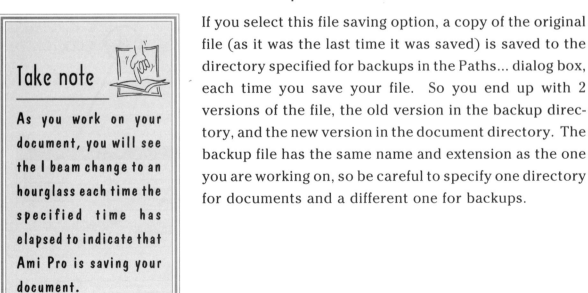

Take note

As you work on your document, you will see the I beam change to an hourglass each time the specified time has elapsed to indicate that Ami Pro is saving your document.

If you select this file saving option, a copy of the original file (as it was the last time it was saved) is saved to the directory specified for backups in the Paths... dialog box, each time you save your file. So you end up with 2 versions of the file, the old version in the backup directory, and the new version in the document directory. The backup file has the same name and extension as the one you are working on, so be careful to specify one directory for documents and a different one for backups.

Saving with a new name

If you've already saved your document and then decided to save it again using a different drive, directory and/or name, you must use **File | Save As....**

You would need to use this option if you want to keep different versions of a file you are working on.

Basic steps

1 Open the **File** Menu

2 Choose **Save As** ...

3 At the **Save As** dialog box, specify the new Drive, Directory and/ or File Name required

4 Click **OK**.

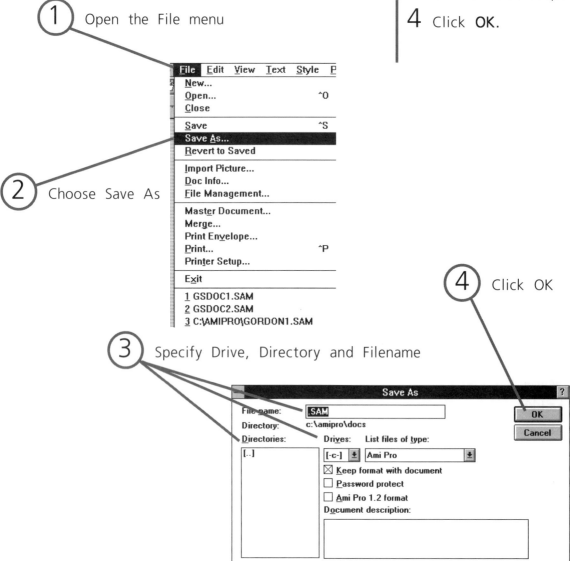

(1) Open the File menu

(2) Choose Save As

(3) Specify Drive, Directory and Filename

(4) Click OK

File	Edit	View	Text	Style	P

New...
Open...   ^O
Close

Save   ^S
Save As...
Revert to Saved

Import Picture...
Doc Info...
File Management...

Master Document...
Merge...
Print Envelope...
Print...   ^P
Printer Setup...

Exit

1 GSDOC1.SAM
2 GSDOC2.SAM
3 C:\AMIPRO\GORDON1.SAM

Save As

File name: .SAM   OK
Directory: c:\amipro\docs   Cancel
Directories: Drives: List files of type:
[..]   [-c-]   Ami Pro

☒ Keep format with document
☐ Password protect
☐ Ami Pro 1.2 format
Document description:

Basic steps

1 Open the **File** Menu

2 Choose **Close**

3 If your file has not been saved, Ami Pro will prompt you. Respond as appropriate.

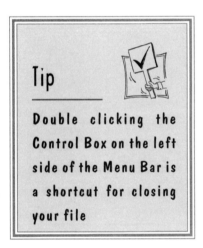

Tip

Double clicking the Control Box on the left side of the Menu Bar is a shortcut for closing your file

Closing a file

Once you have typed up your file, saved and perhaps printed it, you need to Close it. A Closed file can be Opened again when you want to work on it.

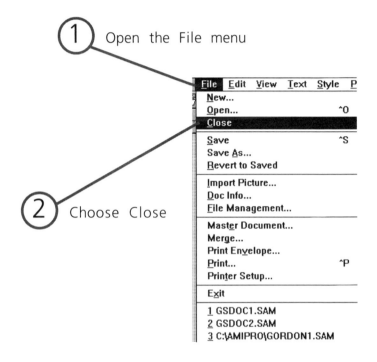

1 Open the File menu

2 Choose Close

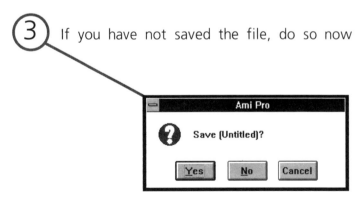

3 If you have not saved the file, do so now

Opening a file

A lot of the time you are working in Ami Pro you will be editing existing documents. To access an existing file you must *open* it. You can then make changes, save and print as required.

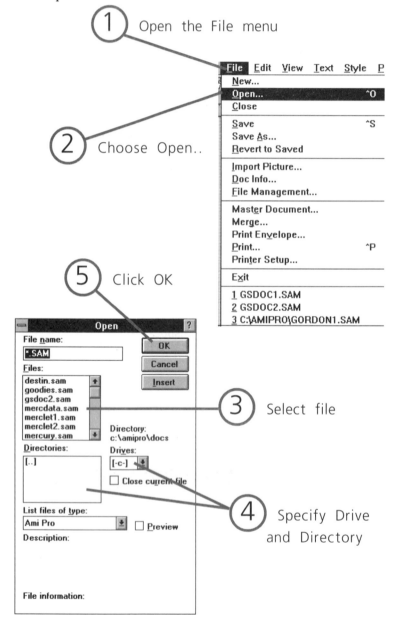

① Open the File menu

② Choose Open..

⑤ Click OK

③ Select file

④ Specify Drive and Directory

Basic steps

1 Open the **File** Menu
2 Choose **Open**
3 Specify the **Drive** and **Directory** that the file is located in
4 Select the required file from the **Files** list
5 Click **OK**

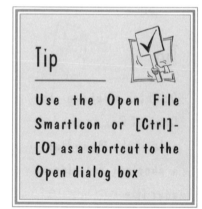

Tip

Use the Open File SmartIcon or [Ctrl]-[O] as a shortcut to the Open dialog box

Tip

In the Open dialog box, double click a file name to Open it.

Basic steps

1 Open the **File** Menu

2 Select **Print**

3 Specify the **Number of copies** required

4 Indicate the **Page Range** (*current* page is the page the insertion point is in when you go to print)

5 Specify **Even**, **Odd** or **Both** pages.

6 Click **OK**

Printing a file

Once your file has been keyed in, checked, edited and saved as required, you will most probably want to print it.

You can print your whole file, individual pages or a range of pages. To print on double-sided, first print the Odd pages, then put the paper back and print the Even pages.

The file you want to print must be open.

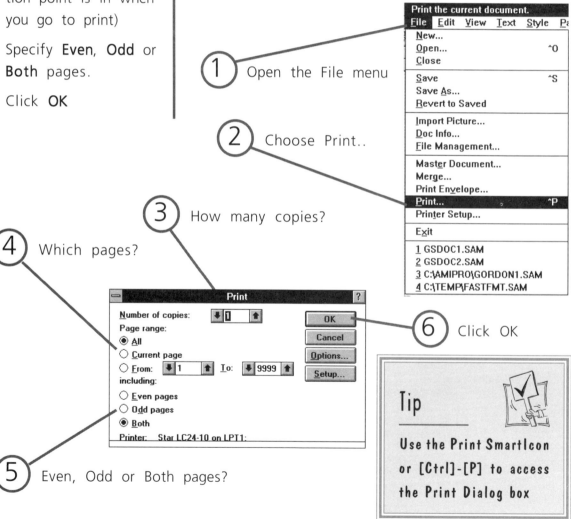

1 Open the File menu

2 Choose Print..

3 How many copies?

4 Which pages?

6 Click OK

5 Even, Odd or Both pages?

Tip

Use the Print SmartIcon or [Ctrl]-[P] to access the Print Dialog box

Summary

- ❑ **File** handling commands include **New, Save, Save As, Close, Open** and **Print**.

- ❑ File handling commands are found in the **File menu**.

- ❑ **SmartIcon shortcuts** can be used for Open, Save and Print.

- ❑ **Auto timed save** can be used to re-save edited documents automatically.

- ❑ **Keyboard shortcuts** can be used for Open ([Ctrl]-[O]), Save ([Ctrl]-[S]) and Print ([Ctrl]-[P])

- ❑ Double click the control box on the menu bar as a shortcut for closing a file.

- ❑ For the most part, the defaults in the dialog boxes will be acceptable.

3 Text entry

Keying in text

Entering text in Ami Pro is very easy. As soon as you are into the application you are all set up ready to type. Things to note are:-

- The insertion point (the vertical, black, flashing character in the document area) indicates where your characters will appear on the screen when you type them in on the keyboard

- The I beam shows you where your mouse is pointing within the text area. When you click the left mouse button, the insertion point moves to where the I beam is.

- DO NOT press the [Enter] key at the end of each typing line - the text will wrap automatically onto the next line. You DO need to press [Enter] at the end of short lines and between paragraphs.

Try keying in the passage opposite.

Basic steps

1 Key in the text
2 Do not press [Enter] at the end of each line. Ami Pro's wordwrap will take the text over to the next line.
3 Press [Enter] at the end of short lines, to mark the end of paragraphs

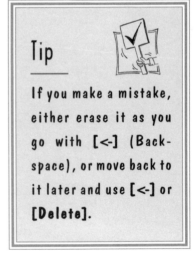

Tip

If you make a mistake, either erase it as you go with [<-] (Back-space), or move back to it later and use [<-] or [Delete].

① Key in text

② Wordwrap

ROYAL DEESIDE

Have a well deserved break in tranquil and picturesque Royal Deeside. Stop over at the four-star Highlander Hotel where you will find an excellent combination of countryhouse charm and modern facilities. The Highlander prides itself on its first class restaurants which serve local game, fish and seafood.

There are also splendid walks, golf, skiing and fishing.

The Highlander also boasts a fully equipt Country Club where you can escape for a swim, sauna, game of squash or tennis. Children can be left in the well supervised play area.

Prices (including breakfast and VAT) start at £89 for a single room and £115 for a double .

③ Press [Enter] at these points

Editing

Once you have keyed in text, you will usually need to edit it in some way. You might want to type more text in, or delete existing text. To do this basic editing, you need to be able to:-

● Move the insertion point to the desired location

● Key in new text

● Delete existing text

● Toggle between insert and typeover mode

Experiment with your text, making the changes indicated, until you have mastered the techniques.

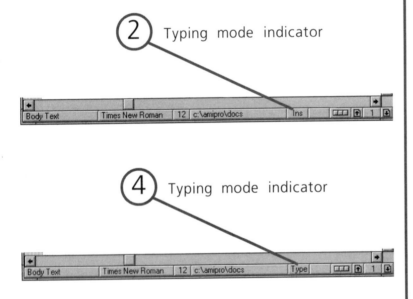

② Typing mode indicator

④ Typing mode indicator

1 Move the insertion point to the desired location - point and click with the mouse or use the cursor keys

2 Key in new text - simply type - the default typing mode is *Insert*. Notice the typing mode button on the Status Bar

3 Delete existing text - if the characters to be deleted are to the right of the insertion point use **[Delete]**, if they are to the left of the insertion point use **[Backspace]**.

4 To type over existing text and replace it, press **[Insert]** (note the mode button on the status bar changes to *Type*). Key in your replacement text. Press **[Insert]** again to get back into *Insert* mode.

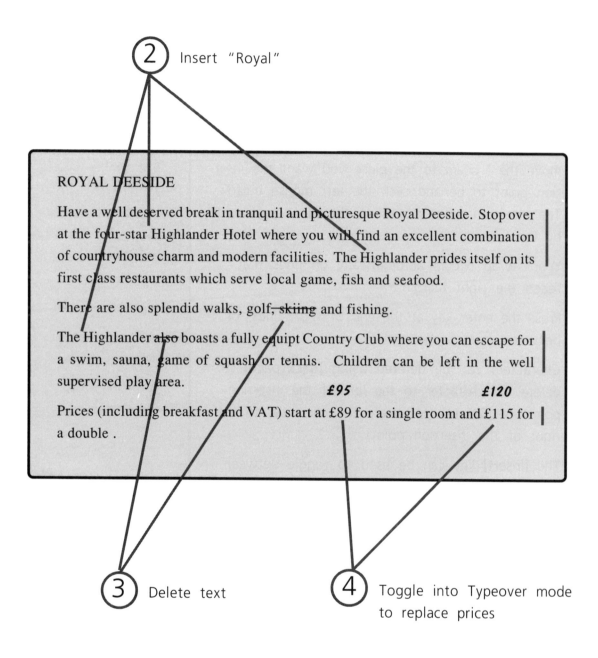

② Insert "Royal"

ROYAL DEESIDE

Have a well deserved break in tranquil and picturesque Royal Deeside. Stop over at the four-star Highlander Hotel where you will find an excellent combination of countryhouse charm and modern facilities. The Highlander prides itself on its first class restaurants which serve local game, fish and seafood.

There are also splendid walks, golf, skiing and fishing.

The Highlander also boasts a fully equipt Country Club where you can escape for a swim, sauna, game of squash or tennis. Children can be left in the well supervised play area.

£95   *£120*

Prices (including breakfast and VAT) start at £89 for a single room and £115 for a double .

③ Delete text

④ Toggle into Typeover mode to replace prices

Summary

❏ The insertion point is the flashing, black, vertical character in the text area.

❏ You can move the insertion point to a new position using the arrow cursor keys

❏ To move the insertion point using the mouse, move the I beam to the place you want the insertion point to be and click the left mouse button. The insertion point moves to the place indicated by the I beam.

❏ Word wrap occurs automatically on lines that reach the right margin.

❏ Press the enter key at the end of short lines, or between paragraphs.

❏ Characters can be deleted using **[Backspace]** (to delete the character to the left of the insertion point) or **[Delete]** (to delete the character to the right of the insertion point)

❏ The **[Insert]** key can be used to toggle between Insert mode (the default) and Typeover mode.

4 Setting text styles

Bold, italics & underline

When creating your documents, you'll often want to draw attention to particular text by highlighting it in some way. There is a vast range of text formatting options available to you with Ami Pro, the most regularly used ones being Bold, Italics and Underline.

Here we consider how you apply these formatting options to text as you key the text in.

Format	Smarticon	Keyboard shortcut
Bold	B	[Ctrl]-[B]
Italic	I	[Ctrl]-[I]
Underline	U	[Ctrl]-[U]

Basic steps

1 Switch on the text formatting option (or options) required using the appropriate SmartIcon (simply point and click the SmartIcon)

2 Key in the text

3 Switch off the text formatting option (or options) using the same SmartIcon again.

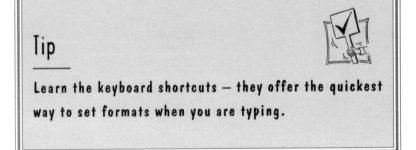

Tip

Learn the keyboard shortcuts — they offer the quickest way to set formats when you are typing.

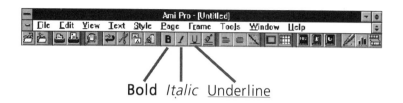

Bold *Italic* <u>Underline</u>

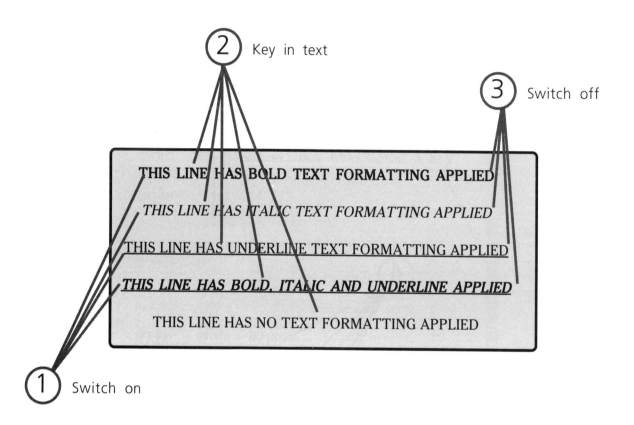

② Key in text

③ Switch off

THIS LINE HAS BOLD TEXT FORMATTING APPLIED

THIS LINE HAS ITALIC TEXT FORMATTING APPLIED

<u>THIS LINE HAS UNDERLINE TEXT FORMATTING APPLIED</u>

<u>THIS LINE HAS BOLD, ITALIC AND UNDERLINE APPLIED</u>

THIS LINE HAS NO TEXT FORMATTING APPLIED

① Switch on

Changing faces

Your font style, or face as Ami Pro calls it, describes the character set you are using to display your text. The face you are using is displayed on the Status Bar. You can change to another face for all or part of your document very easily.

Basic steps

1 Click the **Face** button on the Status Bar

2 Scroll up or down the list until you see the **Font name** you want to use

3 Click on the Font name to select it

4 Key in the text you want in this Font

5 Repeat steps 1-4 to change Font as required

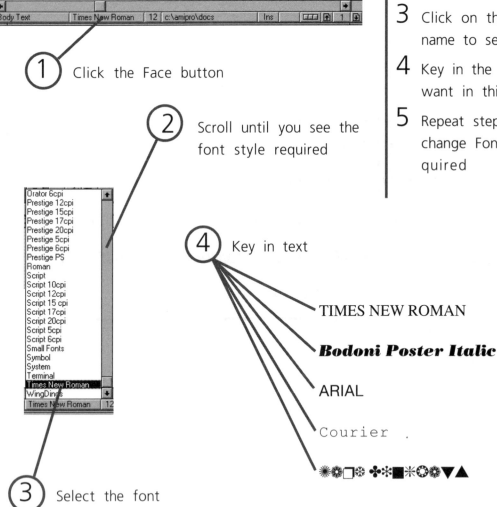

Click the Face button

Scroll until you see the font style required

Key in text

Select the font

TIMES NEW ROMAN

Bodoni Poster Italic

ARIAL

Courier

Basic steps

1 Click the **Size** button on the Status Bar

2 Select the size

3 Key in your text

4 Repeat steps 1-3 to change the character size as necessary

Setting the size

There will be times when you want to vary the size of characters you type in, for headings for example, or to add emphasis to some text. This can be done using the Size button on the Status Bar.

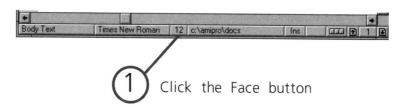

| Body Text | | Times New Roman | 12 | c:\amipro\docs | | Ins | | 1 |

(1) Click the Face button

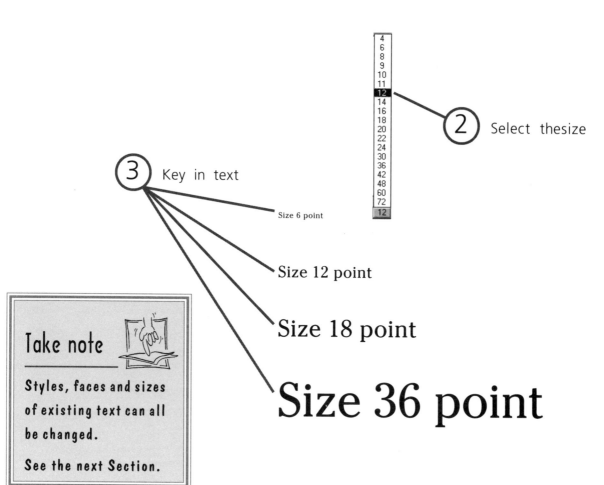

(2) Select thesize

(3) Key in text

Size 6 point

Size 12 point

Size 18 point

Size 36 point

Take note

Styles, faces and sizes of existing text can all be changed.

See the next Section.

Summary

❑ Text can easily be formatted as it is keyed in.

❑ The quickest way to make text bold, italic or underlined is to use the SmartIcons or the keyboard shortcuts [Ctrl]-[B], [Ctrl]-[I] and [Ctrl]-[U].

❑ The SmartIcons and keyboard shortcuts are **toggles** - they switch the formatting on or off.

❑ The **Face** button on the status bar can be used to change the font style.

❑ The **Size** button on the status bar can be used to change the font size.

❑ To format text as it is keyed in the sequence is - switch on or choose the format, key in the text, switch off or choose the next format.

5 Formatting text

Selecting text

Once you have typed your text in, you can SELECT the text and then change it in a number of ways. By selecting existing text, you can then make changes to it without having to re-type it. You can:-

● edit the text formatting of selected text

● delete selected text

● replace selected text

● move or copy selected text

There are a number of ways to select text. Three are shown here. Try them to select any amount of text - a word, a few words, a few paragraphs etc.

Useful Keyboard Selection Techniques

To select from the insertion point to the end of the document press **[Shift]-[Ctrl]-[End]** (Move the insertion point to the beginning if you want all of the file).

To select from the insertion point to the end of the line press **[Shift]-[End]** (Move the insertion point to the beginning of the line first, if you want it all).

{Shift}-[Ctrl]-[Home] and [Shift]-[Home] work backwards from the insertion point, to the beginning to the document or line respectively.

❑ **Click**

1 Put the insertion pointanywhere in the text to be selected

2 **Double-Click** to select the surrounding word

❑ **Shift - Click**

1 Put the insertion point at the beginning (or end) of the text to be selected

2 Move the I beam to the other end

3 Hold down **[Shift]** and click the left mouse button

☐ Click and Drag

1 Position the I beam at the beginning or the end of the text to be selected.

2 Hold down the left mouse button, and drag over the required text.

Tip

Click and Drag can also be used to select any unit of text. If you select the wrong text, simply click anywhere in the text area to de-select, and try again.

① Put insertion point at one end of the text

ROYAL DEESIDE

Have a well deserved break in tranquil and picturesque Royal Deeside. Stop over at the four-star Royal Highlander Hotel where you will find an excellent combination of countryhouse charm and modern facilities. The Royal Highlander prides itself on its first class restaurants which serve local game, fish and seafood.

There are also splendid walks, golf and fishing.

The Royal Highlander boasts a fully equipt Country Club where you can escape for a swim, sauna, game of squash or tennis. Children can be left in the well supervised play area.

Prices (including breakfast and VAT) start at £95 for a single room and £120 for a double .

---

② Move the I beam to the other end

③ Hold [Shift] and click

Undoing mistakes

Selected text can be edited and moved around in many ways. It can also be replaced (by typing through the keyboard when you have text selected) or deleted (by pressing [**Delete**] or [**Backspace**] when you have text selected) – intentionally or unintentionally!!

Should you delete or replace selected text *unintentionally*, don't panic! **Undo** should save the situation most of the time.

To check if Undo is switched on, try it and see, or open the **Edit** menu and see if the **Undo** option is dimmed (switched off) or not.

☐ **To Undo an action**

1 Click the **Undo** SmartIcon

or

1 Press [**Ctrl**]-[**Z**]

or

1 Open the **Edit** menu

2 Choose **Undo**

3 Repeat if necessary to undo previous actions (up to the number of levels set).

① Open the Edit menu

Edit	View	Text	Sty
Undo			^Z
Cut			^X
Copy			^C
Paste			^V
Paste Link			
Paste Special...			
Link Options...			
Find & Replace...		^F	
Go To...		^G	
Insert			▶
Power Fields			▶
Mark Text			▶
Bookmarks...			

② Choose Undo

Ami Pro - [Untitled]

File Edit View Text Style Page Frame Tools Window Help

① Undo Smarticon

Basic steps

❑ **To switch Undo on/off** or change the number of levels:-

1 Open the **Tools** Menu

2 Choose **User Setup..**

3 Drop down the list of **Undo level** options

4 Specify the number of levels required

5 Click **OK**

Setting the Undo level

You can have between 1 and 4 Undo levels, or turn the feature off completely. The higher the level number, the more changes you can Undo.

Level 1 is enough for many people. This lets you Undo the change that you just made by mistake – such as the block of text that you deleted when you were trying to set its font style!

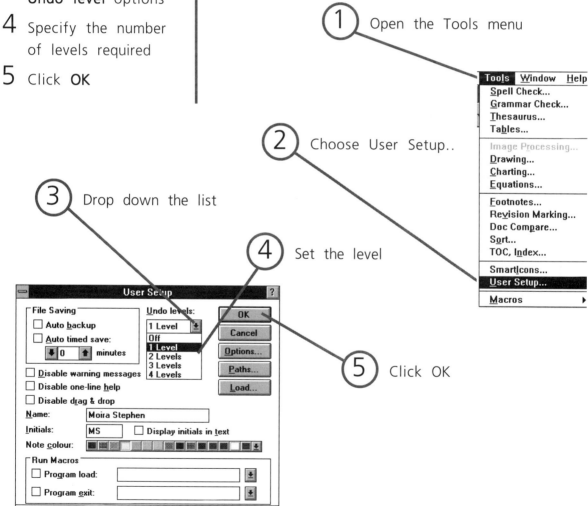

① Open the Tools menu

② Choose User Setup..

③ Drop down the list

④ Set the level

⑤ Click OK

Formatting existing text

Basic steps

Formatting existing text is easy as long as you know how to select text and know how to apply the required formatting. You might want to make existing text bold, italic or underlined, or to change the font style or size.

Selecting text was covered earlier in this section.

Applying a format to existing text is done in the same way as selecting a format for new text. (See Section 4.)

● Experiment on existing text.

1 Select the text to be formatted

2 Apply the formatting required

3 Deselect the text

 1 Select the text

ROYAL DEESIDE

Have a well deserved break in tranquil and picturesque Royal Deeside. Stop over at the four-star *Royal Highlander Hotel* where you will find an excellent combination of countryhouse charm and modern facilities. *The Royal Highlander* prides itself on its first class restaurants which serve local game, fish and seafood.

There are also splendid walks, golf and fishing.

The *Royal Highlander* boasts a fully equipt Country Club where you can escape for a swim, sauna, game of squash or tennis. Children can be left in the well supervised play area.

Prices (including breakfast and VAT) start at £95 for a single room and £120 for a double .

---

 2 Apply formatting

Deselect the text

ROYAL DEESIDE

Have a well deserved break in tranquil and picturesque **Royal Deeside**. Stop over at the four-star *Royal Highlander Hotel* where you will find an excellent combination of countryhouse charm and modern facilities. *The Royal Highlander* prides itself on its first class restaurants which serve local game, fish and seafood.

There are also splendid walks, golf and fishing.

The *Royal Highlander* boasts a fully equipt Country Club where you can escape for a swim, sauna, game of squash or tennis. Children can be left in the well supervised play area.

Prices (including breakfast and VAT) start at £95 for a single room and £120 for a double .

Tip

Always remember to deselect the block of text before doing anything else. If you forget, the results can be highly unpredictable.

Changing text formats

Sometimes you will find that you do not like the way you have formatted your text and you decide to remove or change the formatting you have applied. This is done in the same way as applying formatting to existing text.

● Experiment on some existing text, changing or removing the formatting.

1 Select the text that has the formatting to be removed or changed

2 Click the **SmartIcon**, use the keyboard shortcut or choose the new font style or size from the list displayed when you click the **Face** or **Size** button

3 De-select the text

 Select the text

② Make the changes

ROYAL DEESIDE

Have a well deserved break in tranquil and picturesque **Royal Deeside**. Stop over at the four-star *Royal Highlander Hotel* where you will find an excellent combination of countryhouse charm and modern facilities. *The Royal Highlander* prides itself on its first class restaurants which serve local game, fish and seafood.

There are also splendid walks, golf and fishing.

The *Royal Highlander* boasts a fully equipt Country Club where you can escape for a swim, sauna, game of squash or tennis. Children can be left in the well supervised play area.

Prices (<u>including breakfast and VAT</u>) start at £95 for a single room and £120 for a double .

3 Deselect the text

ROYAL DEESIDE

Have a well deserved break in tranquil and picturesque **Royal Deeside**. Stop over at the four-star *Royal Highlander Hotel* where you will find an excellent combination of countryhouse charm and modern facilities. *The Royal Highlander* prides itself on its first class restaurants which serve local game, fish and seafood.

There are also splendid walks, golf and fishing.

The *Royal Highlander* boasts a fully equipt Country Club where you can escape for a swim, sauna, game of squash or tennis. Children can be left in the well supervised play area.

Prices (<u>including breakfast and VAT</u>) start at £95 for a single room and £120 for a double .

Tip

If text has several formatting options applied to it, and you want to remove them all, select it and use [Ctrl]-[N] to return it to Normal.

Copying a format

A very useful tool when using the same formatting on several pieces of text in your document is **Fast Format**. Fast Format allows you to copy the **text** formatting from one piece of text and apply it to other areas.

Basic steps

1 Select the text that has the formatting you want to copy

2 Click the **Fast Format** SmartIcon or use the menu option

   File | Fast Format

(Note the Fast Format mouse pointer)

② Click Fast Format

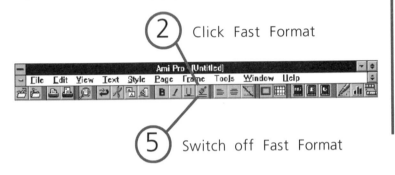

⑤ Switch off Fast Format

① Select the text

③ Click and drag over text

WALKING HOLIDAYS

A walking holiday is the perfect way to get away from it all and enjoy some exercise, fresh air and spectacular scenery. Most walks are carefully graded so you can choose the pace and terrain that suits you.

There's a wide range of destinations to suit all tastes - choose from the picturesque landscapes of the <u>Scottish glens</u>, a climb up to the <u>Everest Base Camp</u> 19,000 feet above daily life in Nepal or a stroll through the blissfully empty <u>country roads of France or Italy</u>.

Take comfortable walking boots, a good picnic, your binoculars and camera and try a walk in your area this weekend!

④ Repeat as necessary

3 Click and drag over the text you want to apply the formatting to

4 Repeat step 3 as often as necessary

5 Click the Fast Format SmartIcon again to cancel

Text after using Fast Format to copy Bold formatting from **walking holiday** to three other phrases.

WALKING HOLIDAYS

A **walking holiday** is the perfect way to get away from it all and enjoy some exercise, fresh air and spectacular scenery. Most walks are carefully graded so you can choose the pace and terrain that suits you.

There's a wide range of destinations to suit all tastes - choose from the picturesque landscapes of the **Scottish glens**, a climb up to the **Everest Base Camp** 19,000 feet above daily life in Nepal or a stroll through the blissfully empty **country roads of France or Italy**.

Take comfortable walking boots, a good picnic, your binoculars and camera and try a walk in your area this weekend!

Changing case

How often are you busy keying in a document, only to look at the screen and realise you've typed half a paragraph in with the [**Caps Lock**] on? No need to worry. You can use the Case Change option to fix things without rekeying the text again.

Basic steps

1 Select the text that you want to change the case of

2 Open the **Text** menu

3 Choose **Caps**

4 Select the option from the list provided

1 Select the text

WALKING HOLIDAYS

A **walking holiday** is the perfect way to get away from it all and enjoy some exercise, fresh air and spectacular scenery. Most walks are carefully graded so you can choose the pace and terrain that suits you.

There's a wide range of destinations to suit all tastes - choose from the picturesque landscapes of the **Scottish glens**, a climb up to the **Everest Base Camp** 19,000 feet above daily life in Nepal or a stroll through the blissfully empty **country roads of France or Italy**.

Take comfortable walking boots, a good picnic, your binoculars and camera and try a walk in your area this weekend!

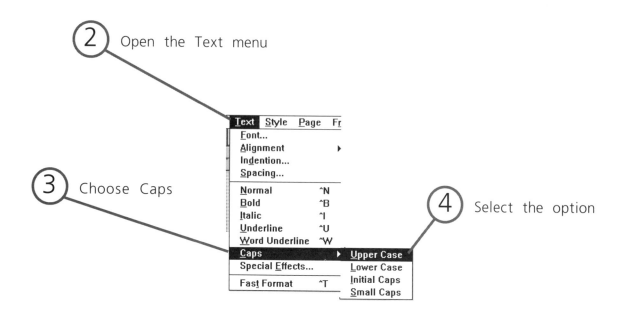

② Open the Text menu

③ Choose Caps

④ Select the option

Text Style Page Fr
Font...
Alignment   ▶
Indention...
Spacing...

Normal   ^N
Bold   ^B
Italic   ^I
Underline   ^U
Word Underline   ^W
Caps   ▶   **Upper Case**
Special Effects...   Lower Case
                      Initial Caps
Fast Format   ^T   Small Caps

WALKING HOLIDAYS

A **walking holiday** is the perfect way to get away from it all and enjoy some exercise, fresh air and spectacular scenery. Most walks are carefully graded so you can choose the pace and terrain that suits you.

There's a wide range of destinations to suit all tastes - choose from the picturesque landscapes of the **Scottish glens**, a climb up to the **Everest Base Camp** 19,000 feet above daily life in Nepal or a stroll through the blissfully empty **country roads of France or Italy**.

Take COMFORTABLE WALKING BOOTS, a good picnic, your binoculars and camera and try a walk in your area this weekend!

Final text

Setting special effects

In addition to the text formatting options most commonly used, you can also create some special effects using Ami Pro.

Subscript and superscript - H_2O and 90^oC

~~Strikethrough~~ effect to mark text for deletion

Double underline money and final totals (£10,000)

Overstrike either ~~using slash~~, or ~~using tilde~~.

Basic steps

1 Select the text
2 Open the **Text** menu
3 Choose

   Special Effects...
4 Select the effect(s) required
5 Click **OK**

(1) Select the text

The final total due is £**125.75** and this should be paid in full by the end of this month.

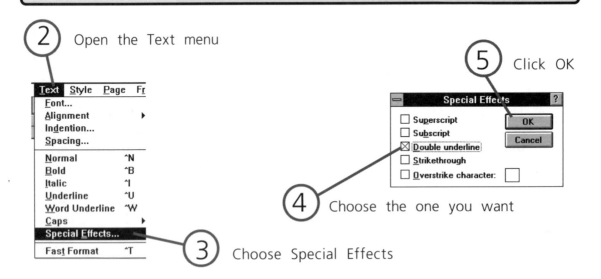

(2) Open the Text menu

(5) Click OK

Text	Style	Page	Fr
Font...			
Alignment		▶	
Indention...			
Spacing...			
Normal		^N	
Bold		^B	
Italic		^I	
Underline		^U	
Word Underline		^W	
Caps		▶	
Special Effects...			
Fast Format		^T	

Special Effects

☐ Superscript
☐ Subscript
☒ Double underline
☐ Strikethrough
☐ Overstrike character: ☐

OK
Cancel

(4) Choose the one you want

(3) Choose Special Effects

The final total due is £125.75 and this should be paid in full by the end of this month.

44

Basic steps

1 Select the text you want to format

2 Open the **Text** menu

3 Choose

Word underline

Word underline

In addition to normal underline and double underline, there may be times you want to underline some text with only the actual words underlined, but not the spaces between the words. Word underline is used for this.

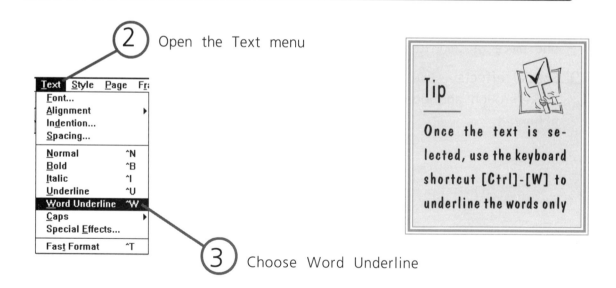

(1) Select the text

Take **COMFORTABLE WALKING BOOTS**, a good picnic, your binoculars and camera and try a walk in your area this weekend!

(2) Open the Text menu

Text	Style	Page	Fra
Font...			
Alignment		▶	
Indention...			
Spacing...			
Normal	^N		
Bold	^B		
Italic	^I		
Underline	^U		
Word Underline	^W		
Caps	▶		
Special Effects...			
Fast Format	^T		

(3) Choose Word Underline

Tip

Once the text is selected, use the keyboard shortcut [Ctrl]-[W] to underline the words only

Take <u>COMFORTABLE</u> <u>WALKING</u> <u>BOOTS</u>, a good picnic, your binoculars and camera and try a walk in your area this weekend!

45

Summary

❏ Existing text must be **selected** before it can be formatted.

❏ Text can be selected in many ways - **Click, Shift-Click** or **Click and Drag** enable you to select any amount of text.

❏ Selected text can be deleted, replaced, moved, copied or formatted.

❏ **Undo** can be used to undo up to the 4th last action (depending on the number of levels you have it set to).

❏ To format existing text the sequence is - Select, format, de-select.

❏ **Fast Format** allows you to copy formatting from one piece of text to another.

❏ **Special effects** - like subscript, superscript, strikethrough and double underline can be easily achieved.

6 Moving and copying

Working within a file

There are 2 methods to choose from when moving or copying things around within a file. These are:-

● Cut or Copy and Paste

● Drag and Drop

Most of the time you can use either technique. However, if you are moving or copying text over long distances Cut or Copy and Paste is probably easier.

Cut   Copy   Paste

1 Select the text to be moved or copied

2 Open the **Edit** menu and select **Cut** (to *move*) or **Copy** (to *copy*) text

3 Reposition the insertion point where the text is to go

4 Open the **Edit** menu and select **Paste** to place the text in its new position

---

Tip

Use the Cut, Copy or Paste Smarticons as a shortcut.

---

(1) Select the text

WALKING HOLIDAYS

A **walking holiday** is the perfect way to get away from it all and enjoy some exercise, fresh air and spectacular scenery. Most walks are carefully graded so you can choose the pace and terrain that suits you.

There's a wide range of destinations to suit all tastes - choose from the picturesque landscapes of the **Scottish glens**, a climb up to the **Everest Base Camp** 19,000 feet above daily life in Nepal or a stroll through the blissfully empty **country roads of France or Italy**.

Take comfortable walking boots, a good picnic, your binoculars and camera and try a walk in your area this weekend!

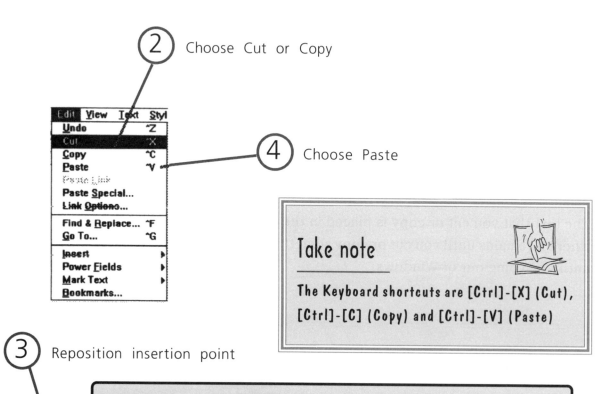

② Choose Cut or Copy

④ Choose Paste

Take note

The Keyboard shortcuts are [Ctrl]-[X] (Cut),
[Ctrl]-[C] (Copy) and [Ctrl]-[V] (Paste)

③ Reposition insertion point

WALKING HOLIDAYS

A **walking holiday** is the perfect way to get away from it all and enjoy some exercise, fresh air and spectacular scenery.

There's a wide range of destinations to suit all tastes - choose from the picturesque landscapes of the **Scottish glens**, a climb up to the **Everest Base Camp** 19,000 feet above daily life in Nepal or a stroll through the blissfully empty **country roads of France or Italy**.

|Most walks are carefully graded so you can choose the pace and terrain that suits you.Take comfortable walking boots, a good picnic, your binoculars and camera and try a walk in your area this weekend!

Cut or Copy?

If you want to *move* something:

    use **Cut** to remove it from its original position

    and **Paste** to insert it into its new position.

If you want to take a *copy* of something to a new position:

    use **Copy** to take a copy of it

    and **Paste** to insert a copy into the new position.

The text that you cut or copy is placed in the *Clipboard*, where it remains until you cut or copy something else, or until you come out of Windows.

Take note

If you need more than one copy of what you have placed in the Clipboard, you can Paste as often as required.

Basic steps

❏ To MOVE text

1 Select the text

2 Position the I beam inside the selected area, hold down the left mouse button, and *drag*

3 Let go of the mouse button at your destination, and the text is *dropped* in

❏ To COPY text

1 Select the text

2 Hold down [Ctrl] the key as you drag.

3 Let go of the mouse button at your destination, and the text is dropped in

Drag and drop

You can also move and copy text inside a file, without using the clipboard. The trick is to drag selected text with the mouse.

The design of the mouse pointer changes when you do this:

 Move

 Copy

❏ Note the mouse pointer shape. Watch the vertical bar at the point which indicates your position

Working between files

You can easily move or copy text between one file and another using the Cut or Copy and Paste techniques.

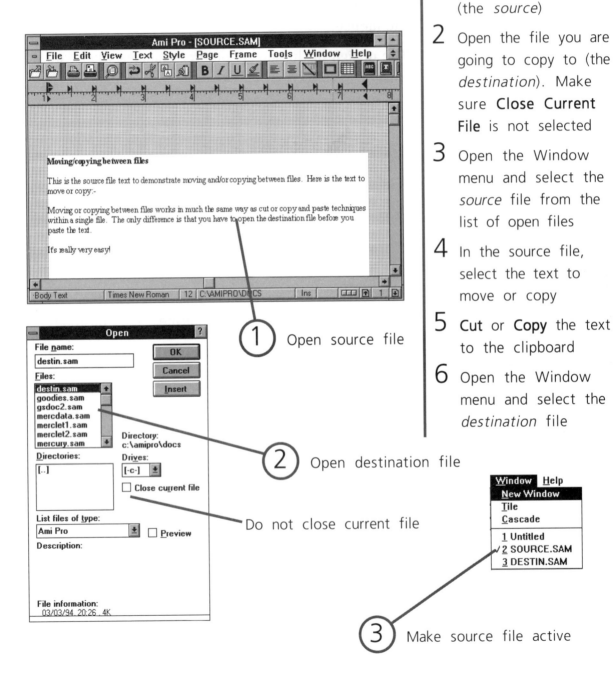

① Open source file

② Open destination file

Do not close current file

③ Make source file active

1 Open the file you are going to copy from (the *source*)

2 Open the file you are going to copy to (the *destination*). Make sure **Close Current File** is not selected

3 Open the Window menu and select the *source* file from the list of open files

4 In the source file, select the text to move or copy

5 **Cut** or **Copy** the text to the clipboard

6 Open the Window menu and select the *destination* file

7 Position the insertion
point where you
want to retrieve the
text

8 **Paste** the text from
the clipboard

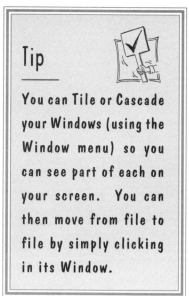

④ Select text

⑤ Cut or Copy

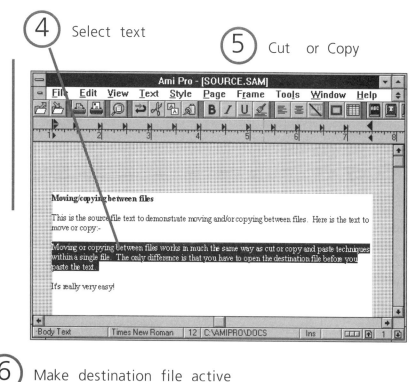

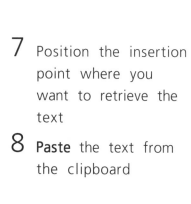

⑥ Make destination file active

⑦ Position insertion point

⑧ Paste

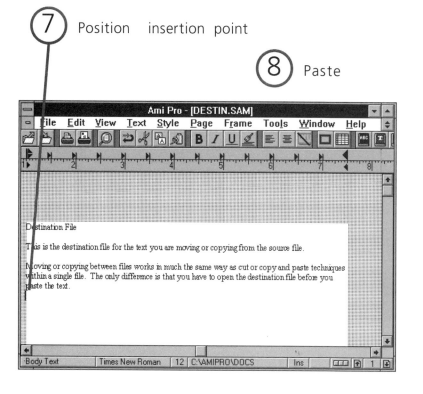

53

Summary

❏ When MOVING text within or between files, you **Cut** it from its original position and then **Paste** it into its new position.

❏ When COPYING text within or between files, you **Copy** it from its original position and then **Paste** it into its new position.

❏ When you use **Cut** or **Copy** from the **Edit** menu, the selected text is placed in the **clipboard**.

❏ The contents of the clipboard can be Pasted as often as required.

❏ The contents of the clipboard remain until something else is cut or copied to the clipboard, or until you exit Windows.

❏ **Drag and Drop** can be used to move or copy within a file, without the selected text being placed in the clipboard.

7 Page layout

Alignment

The alignment, or justification, of your text relative to the margins can be specified using the alignment options.

The default alignment is **Left** - your text is flush with the left margin and you get a ragged right margin where wordwrap occurs.

The alignment can be set to:-

- Left
- Centre
- Right
- Justify (with text flush with both margins)

1 Select the paragraph(s) to be aligned

2 Open the **Text** menu

3 Choose **Alignment**

4 Point and click on the alignment option required

5 Deselect the text

Tip

Use the Left and Centre Smarticons as shortcuts.

Left Centre

(1) Select paragraphs

WALKING HOLIDAYS

A **walking holiday** is the perfect way to get away from it all and enjoy some exercise, fresh air and spectacular scenery. Most walks are carefully graded so you can choose the pace and terrain that suits you.

There's a wide range of destinations to suit all tastes - choose from the picturesque landscapes of the **Scottish glens**, a climb up to the **Everest Base Camp** 19,000 feet above daily life in Nepal or a stroll through the blissfully empty **country roads of France or Italy**.

Take COMFORTABLE WALKING BOOTS, a good picnic, your binoculars and camera and try a walk in your area this weekend!

Selecting paragraphs

The alignment options are *paragraph* formatting commands. This means that they will affect the whole of the paragraph the insertion point is in.

To align ONE paragraph, simply make sure the insertion point is somewhere within in.

To align a set of paragraphs, select them first using the Click, Shift-Click method, or Click and Drag.

① Open Text menu

② Choose Alignment

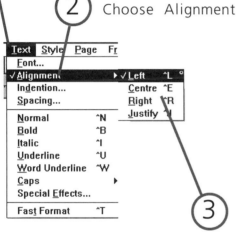

③ Choose the style

Take note

The keyboard shortcuts are [Ctrl]-[L] (Left), [Ctrl]-[E] (Centre), [Ctrl]-[R] (Right) and [Ctrl]-[J] (fully Justified).

WALKING HOLIDAYS

A **walking holiday** is the perfect way to get away from it all and enjoy some exercise, fresh air and spectacular scenery. Most walks are carefully graded so you can choose the pace and terrain that suits you.

There's a wide range of destinations to suit all tastes - choose from the picturesque landscapes of the **Scottish glens**, a climb up to the **Everest Base Camp** 19,000 feet above daily life in Nepal or a stroll through the blissfully empty **country roads of France or Italy**.

Take <u>COMFORTABLE WALKING BOOTS</u>, a good picnic, your binoculars and camera and try a walk in your area this weekend!

Margins

Margins determine the amount of space between the edge of your paper and your text area. You have a top, bottom, left and right margin. The default margins are 1" all round. You can change the margins using the ruler or the Modify Page Layout dialog box.

Your new left and right margins will apply to your whole document, regardless of where the insertion point is when you set them.

The Ruler

Use this to set right and left margins only.

1 Click and drag the black triangles on the lower part of the ruler to the new position (you must click and drag the point of the triangle)

2 Press [Esc] or point and click anywhere in the text area to return to your document

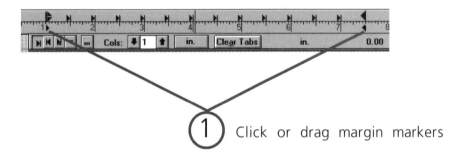

① Click or drag margin markers

② Press [Esc] or click on the text area once set

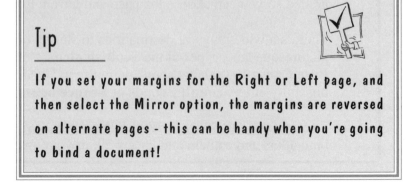

Tip

If you set your margins for the Right or Left page, and then select the Mirror option, the margins are reversed on alternate pages - this can be handy when you're going to bind a document!

Basic steps

1 Open the **Page** menu
2 Select **Modify Page Layout**
3 Make sure that the **Margins & columns** option is selected
4 Specify the **Margins** in the margin fields
5 Indicate which **pages** (All, Right or Left) to apply the margins to
6 Click **OK**

Modify Page Layout dialog box

Use this longer method when you want to set some or all of the top, bottom, left and right margins.

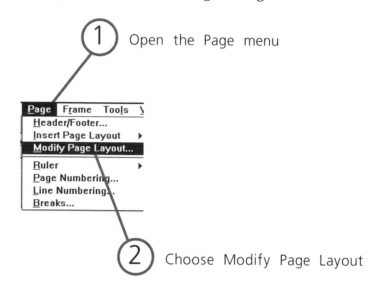

① Open the Page menu

② Choose Modify Page Layout

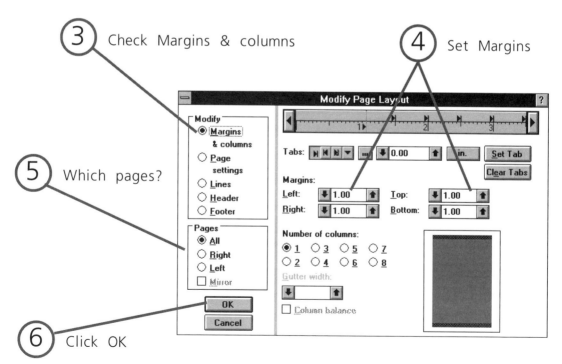

③ Check Margins & columns

④ Set Margins

⑤ Which pages?

⑥ Click OK

Indents

Indents determine the amount of space between the left and/or right margins and the text. You will probably want your text running from margin to margin most of the time, but there will be times you want to indent it to draw attention to it. Using the ruler or the Indention dialog box you can specify the:-

- Left indent of the first line in a paragraph

- Left indent of all lines in a paragraph

- Left indent of all lines except the first line

- Right indent for all lines in a paragraph

Indents are **paragraph** formatting commands. If you insertion point is anywhere in a paragraph when you change the indents, the paragraph the insertion point is in will be affected. If you want to affect several consecutive paragraphs, select them first.

② Set Right marker

③ Return to text

① Drag the Left markers .....

| Cols: ▼ 1 ▲ | in. | Clear Tabs | in. | 0.00 |

❑ **First line only**

Drag upper indent marker only - point to the TIP of the triangle

❑ **All lines**

Drag both indent markers - point to the vertical bar behind the triangles

❑ **All except the first**

Drag just the lower indent marker - point to the TIP of the triangle

Basic steps

☐ **Dialog box**

1 Open the **Text** Menu

2 Select **Indention**

3 Specify the indent required from left and right margins

4 Click **OK**

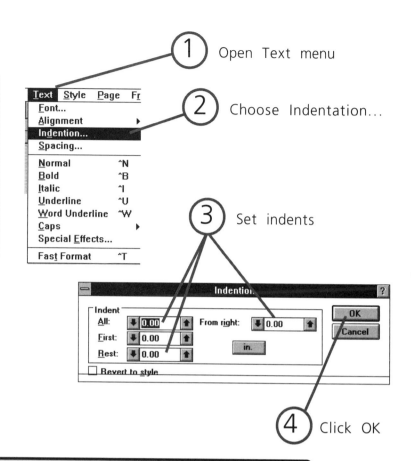

① Open Text menu

② Choose Indentation...

③ Set indents

④ Click OK

DIFFERENT EFFECTS CREATED USING INDENTS

This paragraph has not been indented from the left or right margin. It runs all the way across the typing line from margin to margin.

          All lines in this paragraph have been indented from the left margin and the right margin.

          This paragraph has not been indented from the right margin. The first line only has been indented from the left margin. This can be achieved by dragging the upper left indent along the ruler or using the Indention dialog box.

This paragraph has not been indented from the right margin. All lines except the first have been indented from the left margin. This can be achieved by dragging the lower left indent along the ruler or using the Indention dialog box.

Tabs

If you have text to align in columns, or need to set positions for references, dates etc, you can set Tabs where needed.

Tabs can be:-

- Left
- Right
- Decimal
- Centre

The default tabs are left tabs, set every half inch. You can see them along the top half of the ruler. Use the defaults if they will do. If not, you will have to set your own.

Tabs are **paragraph** formatting commands. If the insertion point is anywhere within a paragraph (line in tab), setting, moving or deleting a tab will affect that paragraph (line) only. To affect several consecutive paragraphs (lines) you will have to select them first.

❏ **Setting Tabs**

1 Click on the Ruler to drop down the lower section (*Tab ruler*)

2 Choose **Clear Tabs** to clear the existing tabs

3 If the tab has to have **leader** dots, click until you see the kind you want - none, underline, hyphens or dots

4 Specify the tab style

5 Point and click on the upper half of the ruler to place the tab

6 To return to the text area, point and click or press **[Esc]**

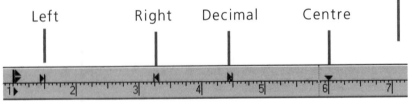

| Left | Right | Decimal | Centre |

Left tabs are	123	12,300.75	These can be useful when
usually used	10	10.00	displaying text
for text	12345	125.60	in a more
entry	1	1,400.25	unusual way

❏ Deleting a Tab

1 Click and drag the tab *down* into the document area

2 Let go the mouse button to *drop* the tab off the ruler

❏ Moving Tabs

1 Click and drag them along the ruler to their new position

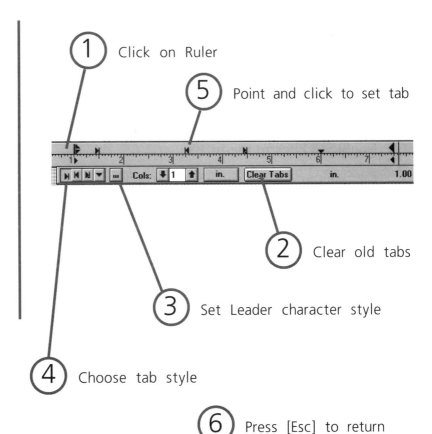

① Click on Ruler

⑤ Point and click to set tab

② Clear old tabs

③ Set Leader character style

④ Choose tab style

⑥ Press [Esc] to return

July 1994	**NEWSLETTER**	Number 20
	Contents	

Note from the Editor - Page 1
New Recruits -Page 3
Refurbishment of Social Club -Page 4
Contract success with France -Page 6

Line spacing

You can modify the line spacing of selected text. Line spacing can be:-

● Single (6 lines to the inch)

● 1° (4 lines to the inch)

● Double (3 lines to the inch)

● Custom (so you can specify the exact line spacing).

Line spacing is a paragraph formatting command.

If the insertion point is anywhere within a paragraph when you modify the line spacing, the whole paragraph takes on the new line spacing.

To modify several consecutive paragraphs, select them first.

Basic steps

1 Open the **Text** menu

2 Select **Spacing**

3 Specify the unit of measurement you want to work with (click on the button to move through alternatives)

4 Select or specify the spacing required.

5 Click **OK**

Take note

Revert to style resets the line spacing to what it was originally (in the paragraph style), before you started messing about with it!!

① Open the Text menu

② Select Spacing

③ Unit of measurement?

④ Set Line spacing

⑤ Click OK

DIFFERENT EFFECTS CREATED USING LINE SPACING

This paragraph is in single line spacing. You get six lines to the inch down the page. Most of the documents you create are likely to be in single line spacing. It is the default spacing - you get single line spacing unless you specify otherwise.

This paragraph is in one and a half line spacing. You

can easily set your text to this spacing using the basic

steps. You get four lines to the inch down the page.

This paragraph is in double line spacing. You get three lines to

the inch in double line spacing. It is very useful for draft

printouts, documents you don't want to look dense with text, or

indeed any documents you want to space out a bit.

Insert page layout

If you do not want your page layout options, the margins and number of columns, applied to all (right or left) pages in your document, you can insert different page layouts for different parts of your document. You might have the first few pages in a single column with 1" margins, then have the next couple of pages with a 2" left margin, and the next few pages in 3 columns.

If you want to use different page layouts for some sections of your document, you must insert a new page layout for each. When you choose to **Insert Page Layout**, Ami Pro moves the insertion point to the top of the next page (unless it is already at the beginning of a page), and the new layout applies from that point forward.

1 Open the **Page** menu

2 Choose **Insert Page Layout**

3 Choose **Insert**

4 Ensure that the **Margins & Columns** modify option is selected

5 Specify the pages that the new layout applies to (all, right or left)

6 Change the margins and number of columns if necessary

7 Click **OK**

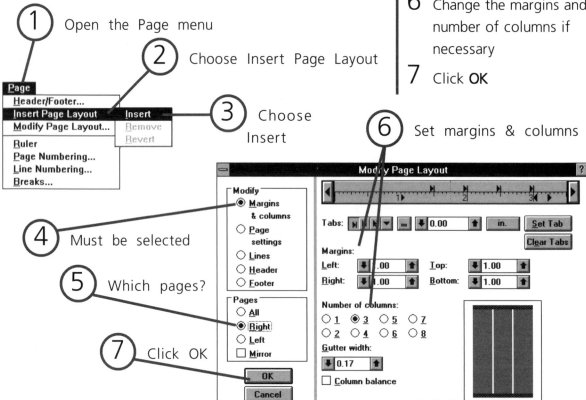

Open the Page menu

Choose Insert Page Layout

Choose Insert

Set margins & columns

Must be selected

Which pages?

Click OK

Removing a page layout

If you insert a new page layout and then decide you do not want to change the page layout, you can easily remove it.

When a page layout is deleted, the insertion point jumps back a page. For example, if you delete the page layout at the top of page 3, the insertion point jumps back to the bottom of page 2.

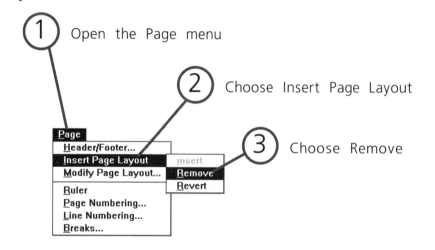

① Open the Page menu

② Choose Insert Page Layout

③ Choose Remove

Page
Header/Footer...
Insert Page Layout
Modify Page Layout...
Ruler
Page Numbering...
Line Numbering...
Breaks...

Insert
Remove
Revert

Summary

- ❑ There are many options that enable you to position text on the page.

- ❑ **Alignment** options allow you to Left, Right, Centre or Fully Justify your text.

- ❑ **Margins** are used to specify the amount of space between the edge of your paper and the main text area.

- ❑ **Indents** are used to specify the amount of space between the margins and the text.

- ❑ **Tabs** can be set to enable you to arrange your input in columns

- ❑ **Tabs** enable you to have text at the left margin, centred and at the right margin on the same line.

- ❑ **Tabs** can be left, right, centre or decimal.

- ❑ **Tabs** can have no **leader** dots, or you can choose from 3 styles of leader dot.

- ❑ **Line Spacing** can be single, one and a half, double or an exact measurement specified by you.

- ❑ To have different page layouts for some sections of your document, you must use **Insert Page Layout**.

8 Useful tools

Help

Now that you are getting into this a bit, where else can you go for Help when you need it? You are lucky, because Ami Pro has a comprehensive On-line Help that can be accessed in a variety of ways. You can get help:-

● From a dialog box when you're not sure how to complete the fields

● Using Point and Shoot

● From the Help Menu

I would recommend either of the first two at this stage.

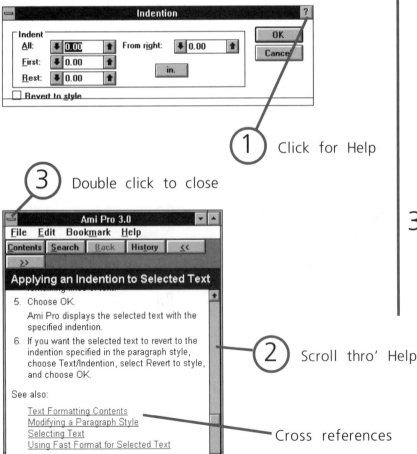

Click for Help

Double click to close

Scroll thro' Help

Cross references

1 Point and click on the Help Button in the top right corner, or press **[F1]**

This takes you into help on the dialog box you were in

2 Scroll through the Help window until you find what you need, accessing cross-references as necessary

The cross-references appear green on most screens. Just point and click at them to access.

3 When you are done, close the Help window, to return to the dialog box

Basic steps

1 Hold **[Shift]** down and press **[F1]** - note the special ? shaped mouse pointer

2 Point and click on the menu you want help on

3 Point and click on the **menu item** you want help on

 You are taken directly to the help you need.

4 When you are finished with Help, close its window to return to your document. The mouse pointer reverts to the normal I beam.

Tip

If you hit **[Shift]-[F1]** by mistake, press **ESC** to return directly to your document.

Point and Shoot Help

Point and Shoot Help is particularly useful for getting help on Menu items. You must be in a document to use Point and Shoot Help.

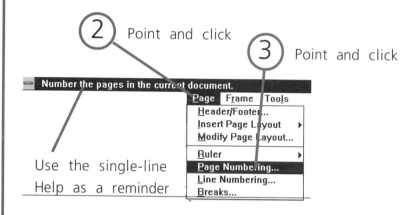

② Point and click

③ Point and click

Use the single-line Help as a reminder

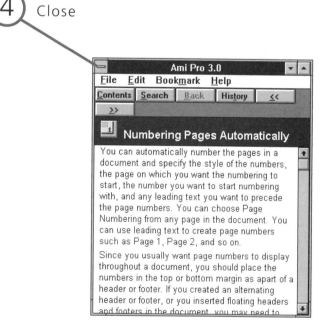

④ Close

Spell check

Spell Checkers are useful tools but beware that they do not pick up every mistake. They are handy for character transposition errors - you type hte instead of the - but they will not pick up a correctly spelt word in the wrong context. If you type "meet" when you mean "meat", spell check cannot help you, "alter" instead of "later" will go undetected! So yes, I would recommend that you always run the spell checker over your documents, but proof read them yourself as well!

Basic steps

1 Click the **Spell Check** SmartIcon

   or

   Open the **Tools** menu and choose

   Spell Check..

2 Complete the dialog box as necessary and choose **OK** to start the checking

3 When an error is found, a dialog box will be displayed - respond as necessary

4 A message **"Spell check complete"** appears briefly at the left of the status bar when the whole document has been checked

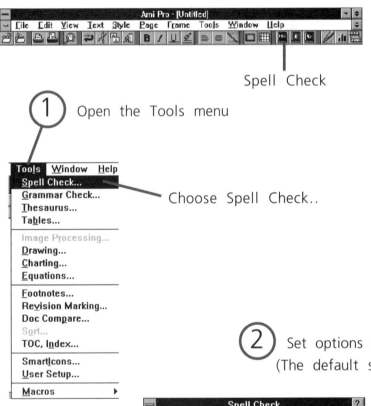

Open the Tools menu

Spell Check

Choose Spell Check..

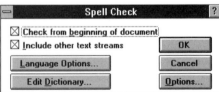

Set options if need be and click OK. (The default settings are usually best)

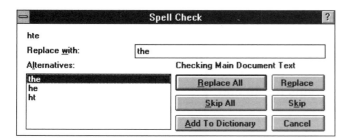

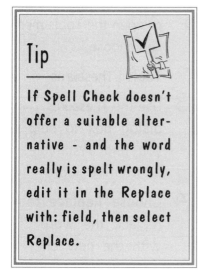

Tip

If Spell Check doesn't offer a suitable alternative - and the word really is spelt wrongly, edit it in the Replace with: field, then select Replace.

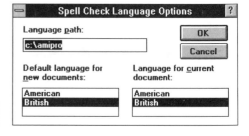

If you have bought additional language dictionaries (there are several available) click this and specify the language you want to use when spell checking your document.

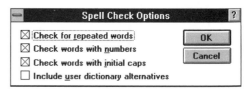

Click this to specify the way Spell Check works

Any time you *add* a word to the dictionary it goes into your User Dictionary. If you want to edit it directly, you can open it using this button. If you are adding words you must press **[Enter]** at the end of ever word you type in. Save the file in the normal way when finished and close it. If you have added a word that has been spelt incorrectly, you can open the User Dictionary and delete it.

Thesaurus

The Thesaurus is very useful when you need a bit of inspiration to find the right word for your document.

It is very easy to interrogate and you have access to 1,400,000 definitions, variations and synonyms for 40,000 root words!!

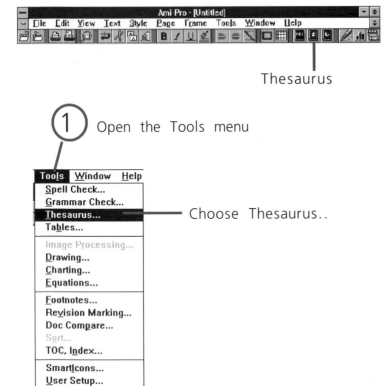

Thesaurus

Open the Tools menu

Choose Thesaurus..

1 Place the insertion point inside the word you want to look up (or select the word)

2 Click the Thesaurus SmartIcon

or open the Tools menu and choose

Tools I Thesaurus

3 Use the **Thesaurus dialog box** to help you find a suitable alternative word

4 Choose **Replace** to replace the word with the new one

or

Cancel if you want to keep the word you are already using

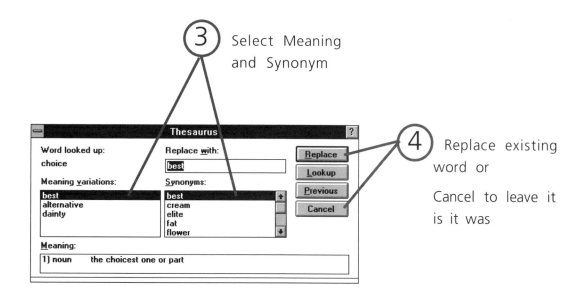

3 Select Meaning and Synonym

4 Replace existing word or

Cancel to leave it is it was

The **Meaning variations** list gives the various meanings attributed to the word you have looked up.

The **Meaning** field at the bottom of the dialog box gives a definition of the word selected in the Meaning variations list.

The **Synonyms** list gives synonyms to the word selected in the Meaning variations list.

Use **LookUp** if you want to list alternatives to the word in the **Replace with:** field, or **Previous** to move back to the last word you looked up.

Find & replace

In addition to moving through your documents using the mouse, cursor keys and scroll bars, Find and Replace can be a useful feature.

You can use the Find and Replace feature:-

● To move the insertion point to a particular location

● To find an occurrence of something and replace it with another - selectively

● To find an occurrence of something and replace it with another - globally

❏ **Find/Selective Replace**

1 Open the **Edit** menu

2 Choose **Find & Re-place**

3 In the **Find** field, key in the text you are trying to Find

4 In the **Replace** field, key in the text you want to replace the Find text with (if any)

5 Choose **Find** to move the insertion point to the first occurrence of the Find text

6 Respond to the dialog box as appropriate

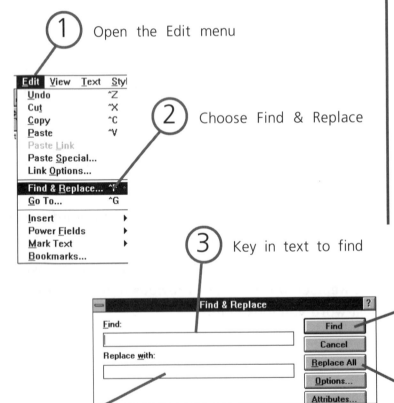

① Open the Edit menu

② Choose Find & Replace

③ Key in text to find

⑤ Find/Selective Replace

See page 78

④ Key in replacement text

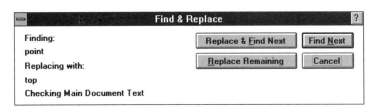

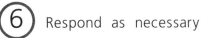

Respond as necessary

❑ **Replace and Find Next** - replaces the find text with the replace text and moves on to find the next occurrence of the find text

❑ **Find Next** - does not replace the find text, but moves on to the next occurrence of it

❑ **Replace Remaining** - replaces all remaining occurrences of the find text with the replace text without prompting you

Options...

Choose this if you need to give additional instructions on Find, Replace, Range and Direction or Type.

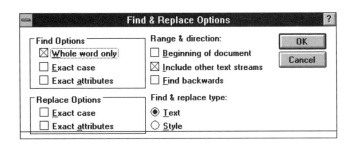

Attributes...

Choose this if you need to specify how the find text is formatted or how the new text should be formatted.

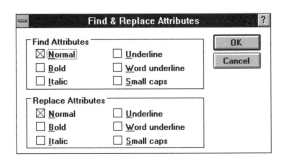

Global Replace

The Global Find and Replace will replace all occurrences of one string of text with another. It is useful where you want to change all references to a particular individual or company with references to another. It can also save repetitive keying of a long company name or technical term. eg your company is called **British Isles Widow and Widower Pension Group** - you could reduce this to BIWWPG (or any unique string of characters) and do a global replace on it when you're done. This way you need only type it in full once.

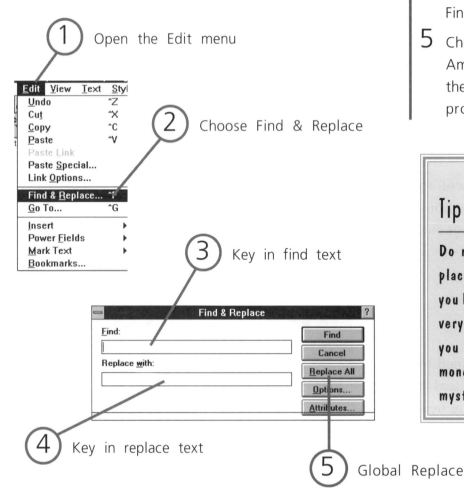

Open the Edit menu

Choose Find & Replace

Key in find text

Key in replace text

Global Replace

1 Open the **Edit** menu

2 Choose **Find & Replace**

3 In the **Find** field, key in the text you are trying to Find

4 In the **Replace** field, key in the text you want to replace the Find text with (if any)

5 Choose **Replace All** Ami Pro completes the task without prompting you.

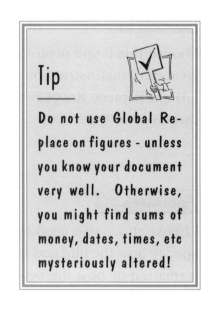

Tip

Do not use Global Replace on figures - unless you know your document very well. Otherwise, you might find sums of money, dates, times, etc mysteriously altered!

Bullets

1 Position the insertion point in your document, where you want the bullet to be

2 Open the **Edit** menu

3 Choose **Insert**

4 Choose **Bullet**

5 Select the Bullet you want to use from the list in the dialog box

6 Click **OK**

If you use (or would like to use) Bullets to emphasise your text, you can do this easily. There are 17 different bullets to select from!

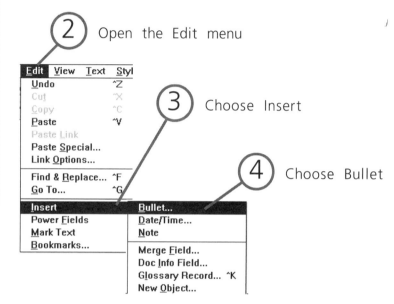

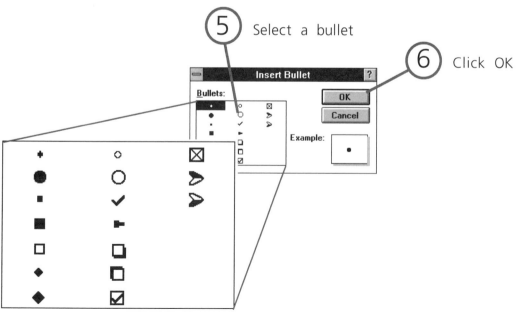

Adding special characters

Basic steps

You can use many "special characters" - some essential, others just for fun, in your documents.

â ç ñ Ü

Ȯ c r

˘ ˚ ∫

👓 ☎ ☺ 💣 👍

To access these special characters, you must run a macro, supplied with Ami Pro, to add another option to the **Edit, Insert** menu. The option is called **Special Characters...**

1. Open the **Tools** menu
2. Choose **Macros**
3. Choose **Playback**
4. Select the Macro *charmap.smm*
5. Click **OK**

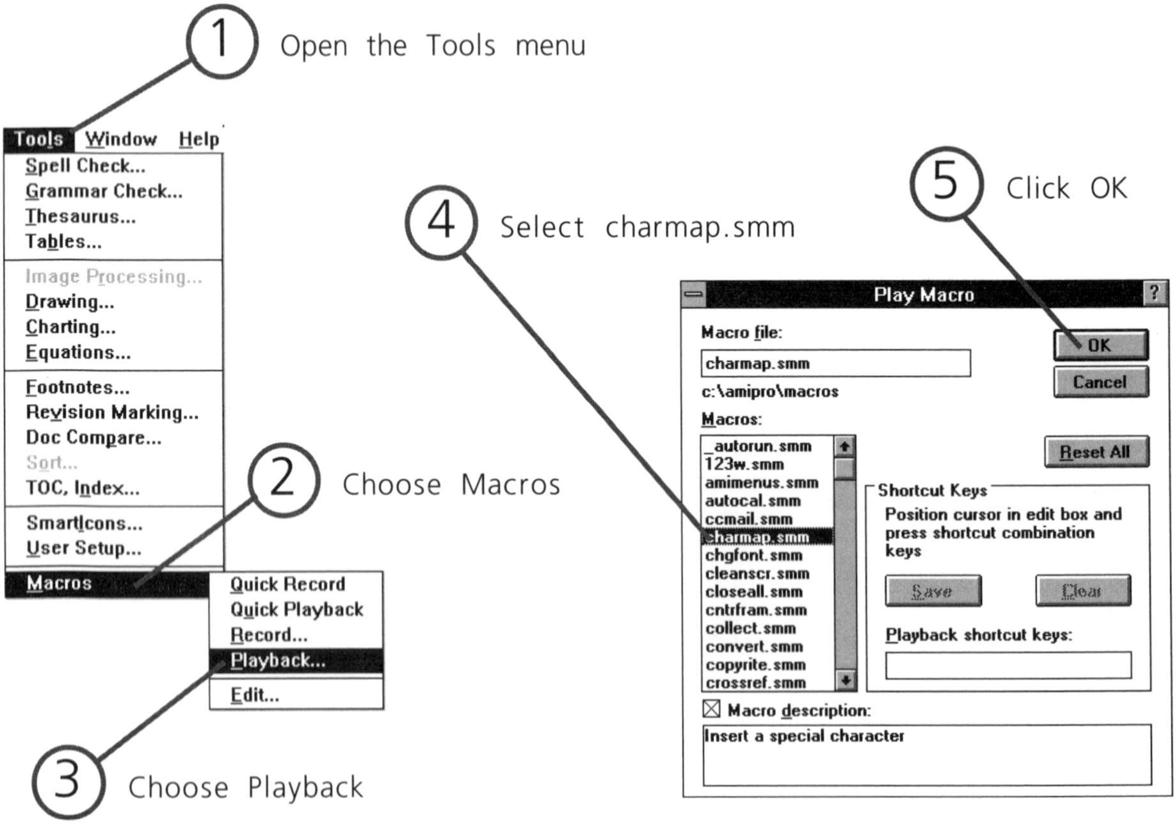

1 Open the Tools menu
Tools Window Help
Spell Check...
Grammar Check...
Thesaurus...
Tables...
Image Processing...
Drawing...
Charting...
Equations...
Footnotes...
Revision Marking...
Doc Compare...
Sort...
TOC, Index...
SmartIcons...
User Setup...
Macros
Quick Record
Quick Playback
Record...
Playback...
Edit...
2 Choose Macros
3 Choose Playback
4 Select charmap.smm
5 Click OK
Play Macro
Macro file:
charmap.smm
c:\amipro\macros
Macros:
_autorun.smm
123w.smm
amimenus.smm
autocal.smm
ccmail.smm
charmap.smm
chgfont.smm
cleanscr.smm
closeall.smm
cntrfram.smm
collect.smm
convert.smm
copyrite.smm
crossref.smm
OK
Cancel
Reset All
Shortcut Keys
Position cursor in edit box and press shortcut combination keys
Save
Clear
Playback shortcut keys:
Macro description:
Insert a special character

Basic steps

1 Open the **Tools** menu
2 Choose **Macros**
3 Choose **Playback**
4 Select the Macro
  _autorun.smm
5 Click **OK**

It takes a minute or
so for Ami Pro to
display the next
dialog box.

6 Choose the special
  character macro from
  the list (the top one)
7 Click **Install**
8 Click **OK**

If you want the **Special Character** option to be added to your **Edit | Insert** menu each time you access Ami Pro you can use another macro to do so.

Each time you access Ami Pro, the macros installed in *Autorun* are executed automatically, so you do not have to go through the procedure manually.

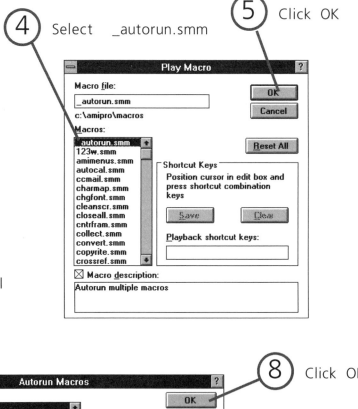

④ Select _autorun.smm

⑤ Click OK

⑥ Choose the special
   character macro

⑧ Click OK

⑦ Click Install

Inserting special characters

You can only select characters from one font at a time - if you need characters from several fonts, you must go through the steps 1-9 for each font required.

If you have difficulty seeing what the characters are, point to a character, click and hold down the left mouse button - the character is enlarged so you can see it clearly.

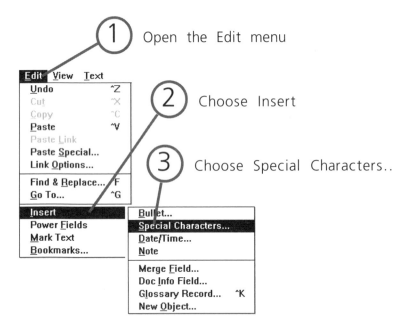

① Open the Edit menu

② Choose Insert

③ Choose Special Characters..

1 Open the **Edit** menu

2 Choose **Insert**

3 Choose **Special Characters...**

4 Select the font that has the character(s) you want to insert

5 Point and click on the character required (a dark border appears around it)

6 Click **Select**

7 Repeat steps 5-6 until you have selected all the characters you want

8 Click **Copy** (this copies the characters to the clipboard)

9 Click **Close**

Tip

Keyboard shortcuts are available for á é í ó ú and ÁÉÍÓÚ. For the lower case letters, hold down [Ctrl] and [Alt] while pressing the letter. For upper case, hold down [Ctrl], [Alt] and [Shift] while pressing the letter.

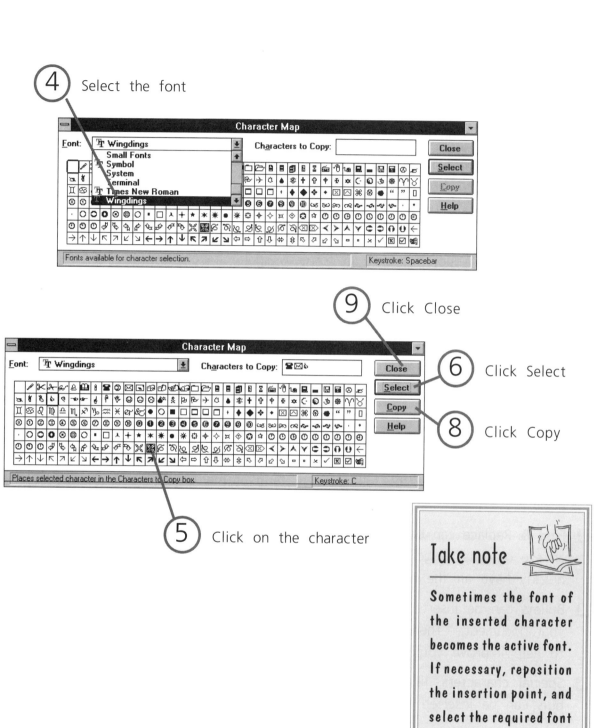

④ Select the font

⑨ Click Close

⑥ Click Select

⑧ Click Copy

⑤ Click on the character

Take note

Sometimes the font of the inserted character becomes the active font. If necessary, reposition the insertion point, and select the required font using the Face button on the Status bar.

Summary

- [ ] Context Sensitive **Help** can be located directly from any dialog box by clicking on the Help button or by pressing [**F1**].

- [ ] Point and Shoot help is accessed by pressing [Shift]-[F1] when you are in a document.

- [ ] **Spell Check** is a useful tool for picking up typing errors. It is *not* a substitute for proof reading however, as it does not pick up correctly spelt words in the wrong context.

- [ ] The **Thesaurus** can help you find the right word for your report.

- [ ] **Find** can be used to move the insertion point to the desired location in your document.

- [ ] **Find & Replace** can be used to automate your work. You can type in a code for your company name or technical term and use Find & Replace to replace the code with the full name or term at the end.

- [ ] **Find & Replace** can be *selective* (so you can keep an eye on what is going on) or *global* (so you can quickly have all the replacements done).

- [ ] **Bullets** can be inserted to highlight key points in your document. There are several to choose from to help improve your presentation.

- [ ] **Special characters**, like foreign letters and symbols can be inserted into your documents.

9 View options

Full page view

When working on a document, the way you look at it is called its View. Usually, the view you work in will be Layout View - the main text area and margin areas are displayed, and about 20 lines in all at any one time.

An alternative, useful, view when working in Layout View is Full Page View, which lets you see a whole page on the screen at a time. It is handy for previewing how your text, white space and graphics (if you are using any) will appear on the page when printed. You would need to have excellent eyesight to be able to read anything, but the full page view can be edited, so you can move/copy things, or change the margins to get your page looking the way you want it.

Full Page / Layout View

② You can edit in this view - it's good for moving paragraphs

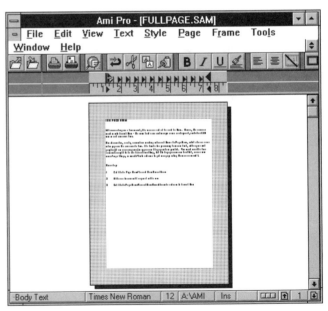

Basic steps

☐ **To Change from Layout Mode to Draft Mode**

1 Open the **View** Menu

2 Choose **Draft Mode**

☐ **To change back again**, open the view menu and choose Layout Mode.

When viewing (or displaying) your document on screen, you have several choices available to you. Usually, you will be in Layout Mode when you view your documents but you might choose to work in Draft Mode instead.

What is the difference?

In **Layout Mode** (the default view mode), you have the main text area and the margin areas (top, bottom, right and left) displayed on the screen. Your document appears on the screen as it will print out. Page breaks, headers, footers and footnotes are all displayed. Layout Mode gives a *WYSIWYG* (What you see is what you get) view of your document.

In **Draft Mode** you get a less formatted view of your document. You see only the main text area - margins, pagebreaks, headers, footers and footnotes are not displayed.

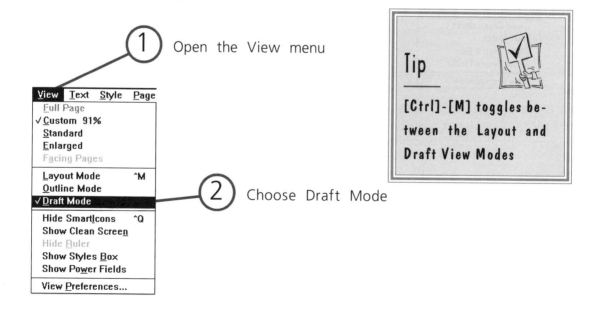

① Open the View menu

② Choose Draft Mode

Tip

[Ctrl]-[M] toggles between the Layout and Draft View Modes

Show/hide SmartIcons

If you want to display as much of your document as possible on the screen at one time, you can clear of some (or most) of the "clutter" to get a better view.

You can elect to show or hide individual elements of the screen or you can "group" the elements you want to show or hide and toggle them on and off as required.

Starting from the top, we have the SmartIcons.

Basic steps

- ❏ **To hideSmartIcons**
- **1** Open the **View** menu
- **2** Choose **Hide SmartIcons** to remove them from the screen
- ❏ **To show SmartIcons**
- **1** Open the **View** menu
- **2** Choose **Show SmartIcons**

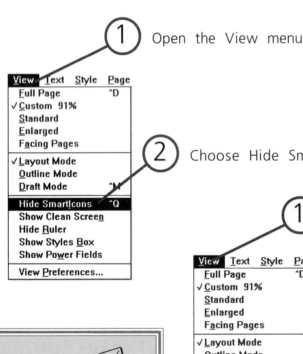

① Open the View menu

② Choose Hide Smarticons

① Open the View menu

② Choose Show Smarticons

Tip

The keyboard shortcut is [Ctrl]-[Q] to toggle between the hide/show SmartIcons option

Show/hide Ruler

❏ **To hide Ruler**

1 Open the **View** menu

2 Choose **Hide Ruler** to remove it from the screen

❏ **To show the Ruler**

1 Open the **View** menu

2 Choose **Show Ruler**

Displaying or hiding the ruler is very similar to displaying or hiding the SmartIcons.

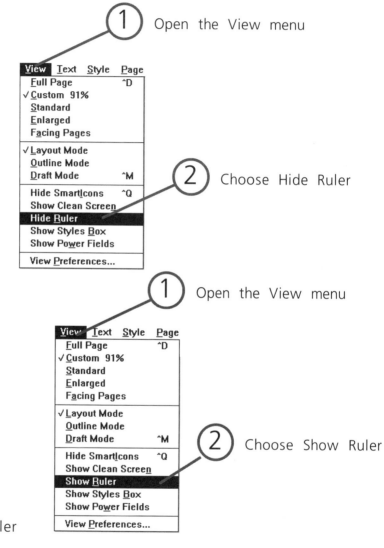

① Open the View menu

② Choose Hide Ruler

① Open the View menu

② Choose Show Ruler

Tip

You can also use the Show/Hide Ruler SmartIcon - it is an on/off toggle

Show/Hide Ruler

The clean screen

If you want to hide or show other elements of the screen, you must firstly specify exactly what you want to display on your "Clean Screen", then choose to view your "Clean Screen" as specified.

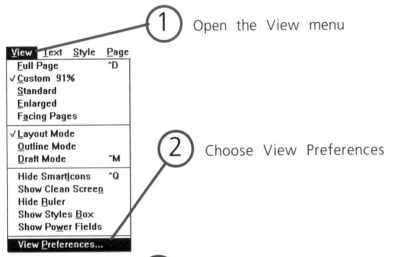

Open the View menu

Choose View Preferences

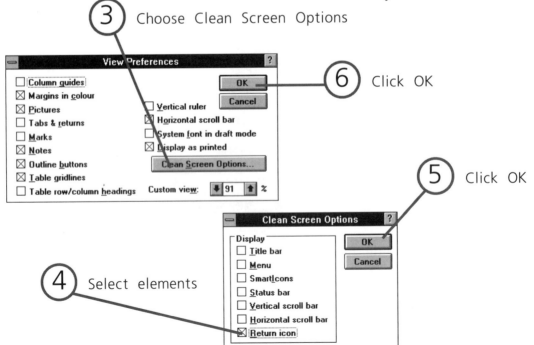

Choose Clean Screen Options

Click OK

Select elements

Click OK

1 Open the **View** Menu

2 Choose **View Preferences...**

3 Choose **Clean Screen Options...**

4 Select the elements you want to display on your "Clean Screen"

5 Click **OK** to return to the **View Preferences...** dialog box

6 Click **OK** to return to your document.

Basic steps

❏ To display your "Clean Screen"

1 Open the **View** menu

2 Choose **Show Clean Screen**

❏ To Hide the Clean Screen

1 Open the **View** menu

2 Choose **Hide Clean Screen**

Show/hide clean screen

Once you have selected your clean screen options, the show/hide toggle is very similar to that of the SmartIcons and Ruler.

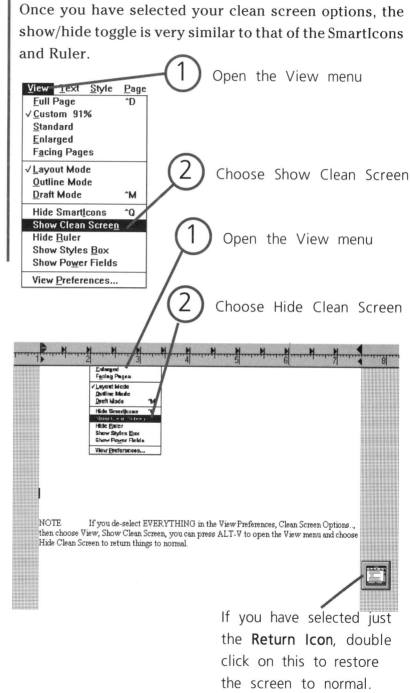

① Open the View menu

② Choose Show Clean Screen

① Open the View menu

② Choose Hide Clean Screen

NOTE   If you de-select EVERYTHING in the View Preferences, Clean Screen Options.., then choose View, Show Clean Screen, you can press ALT-V to open the View menu and choose Hide Clean Screen to return things to normal.

If you have selected just the **Return Icon**, double click on this to restore the screen to normal.

Summary

❑ Different views of your document will be required depending on what you are working on.

❑ **Full Page View** is useful when you want to see how your text, graphics and white space appear on the page.

❑ You can edit while in **Full Page View**.

❑ **Draft Mode** shows your document without its margins, headers, footers, page breaks and page numbering.

❑ **Layout Mode** shows your document with its margins, headers, footers, page breaks and page numbering.

❑ You can choose whether to **show** or **hide** Smarticons, Rulers and other screen elements.

10 Multi-page documents

Page numbering

You can have your pages numbered automatically, while specifying the position for the page number and the style of page numbering to be used. You can:-

● Select from a range of numbering styles

● Specify the page to start numbering on

● Specify the number to start numbering with

● Key in leading text of your choice so you can have Page 1, Page 2 etc

Your Page numbers can be placed in the top or bottom margin, and can be at the left, right or centre of the page. You can be on any page when you set the numbering for the document.

1 If you are not in Layout View, choose **View | Layout Mode** to go into it

2 Place the insertion point in the top or bottom margin area, where you want the Page Numbering to appear. Note the centre tab and the right tab so you can easily position the page number at the left, the centre or the right of the page.

3 Open the **Page** menu and select **Page Numbering**

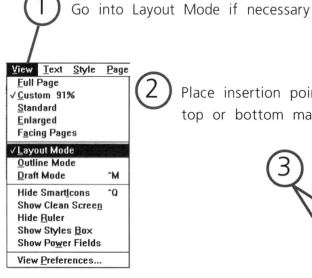

① Go into Layout Mode if necessary

② Place insertion point in top or bottom margin

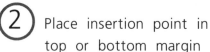

③ Choose Page | Page Numbering..

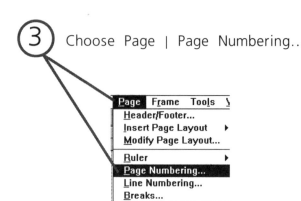

4 Specify the **Style** of numbering required

5 Edit the **Start on page** field if it does not start on the current page

6 Edit the **Start with number** field if necessary

7 Key in any **Leading text** required - ie *Page*

8 Click **OK**

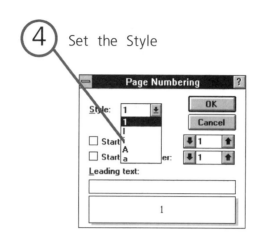

④ Set the Style

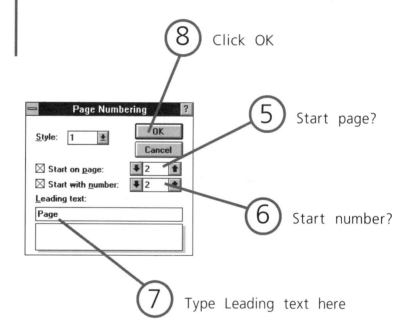

⑧ Click OK

⑤ Start page?

⑥ Start number?

⑦ Type Leading text here

Headers

Headers appear at the top of each page in a document. They are useful for things like references or report titles.

- You must be in **Layout Mode** to insert a header.

- You can be on any page of your document when you insert the header - it will appear on all pages.

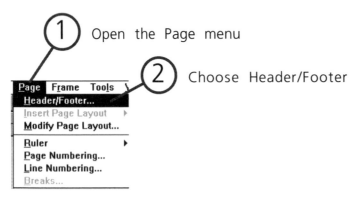

Open the Page menu

Choose Header/Footer

```
Page  Frame  Tools
Header/Footer...
Insert Page Layout    ▶
Modify Page Layout...
Ruler                 ▶
Page Numbering...
Line Numbering...
Breaks...
```

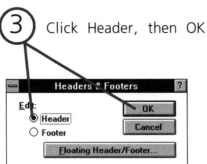

Click Header, then OK

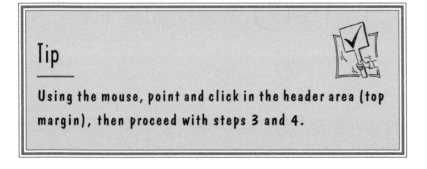

```
Headers & Footers          ?
Edit:                 ┌──────────┐
  ● Header            │    OK    │
                      └──────────┘
  ○ Footer            ┌──────────┐
                      │  Cancel  │
                      └──────────┘
          ┌─────────────────────────┐
          │ Floating Header/Footer... │
          └─────────────────────────┘
```

Tip

Using the mouse, point and click in the header area (top margin), then proceed with steps 3 and 4.

Basic steps

- ☐ **To insert a header**

1 Open the **Page** menu

2 Choose

   Header/Footer...

3 Choose the **Header** option and click **OK**

4 Key in the text you want to appear in the header (note the centre and right tabs on the typing line so you can easily left, centre or right align your header)

5 Press **[Esc]** or point and click in the main text area to return the insertion point to the document area

❏ To delete a header

Simply select the header text (on any page) and press [Delete].

④ Type in Header text

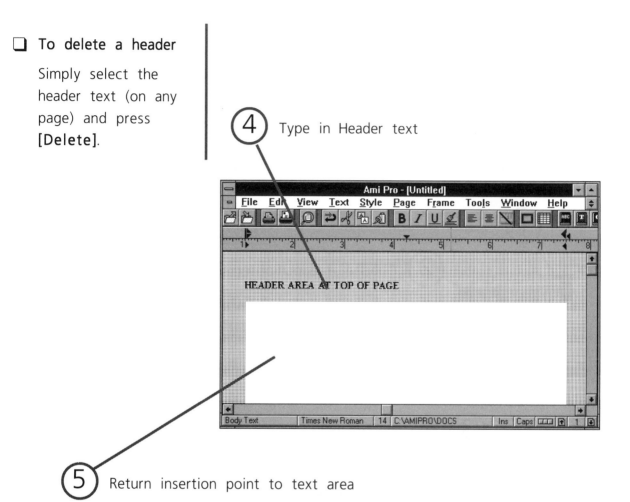

⑤ Return insertion point to text area

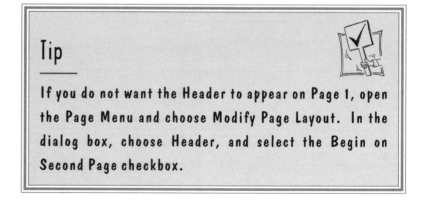

Tip

If you do not want the Header to appear on Page 1, open the Page Menu and choose Modify Page Layout. In the dialog box, choose Header, and select the Begin on Second Page checkbox.

Footers

Footers appear at the bottom of each page in a document. They are useful for things like author's name and/or department.

● You must be in **Layout Mode** to insert a footer.

● As with Headers, you can be on any page of your document when you insert the footer - it will appear on all pages.

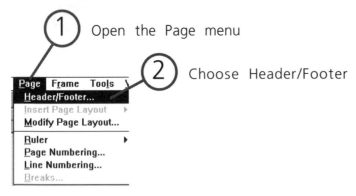

① Open the Page menu

② Choose Header/Footer

③ Click Footer, then OK

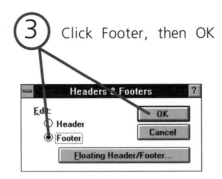

Basic steps

❑ **To insert a footer**

1 Open the **Page** menu

2 Choose **Header/Footer...**

3 Choose the **Footer** option and click **OK**

4 Key in the text you want to appear in the footer (using the centre and right tabs on the typing line to align your footer)

5 Press **[Esc]** or point and click in the main text area to return the insertion point to the document area

---

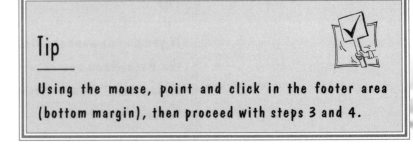

Tip

Using the mouse, point and click in the footer area (bottom margin), then proceed with steps 3 and 4.

To delete a footer

Simply select the footer text (on any page) and press [Delete].

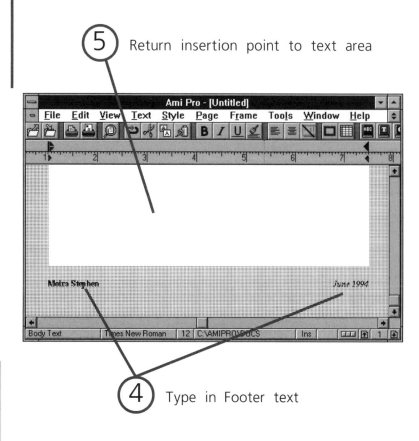

(5) Return insertion point to text area

(4) Type in Footer text

Tip

If you do not want the Footer to appear on Page 1, open the Page Menu and choose Modify Page Layout. In the dialog box, choose Footer, and select the Begin on Second Page checkbox.

Page breaks

When keying text into your documents, page breaks occur automatically when you reach the end of each page. There will, however, be times when you want to control exactly where a page break will happen:-

● When you want to start a section of a report on a new page

● When you are typing several memos or letters into one file, and want each one to start on a new page

① Place the insertion point where you want the page break

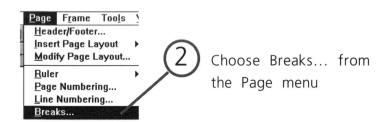

② Choose Breaks... from the Page menu

③ Select Insert page break

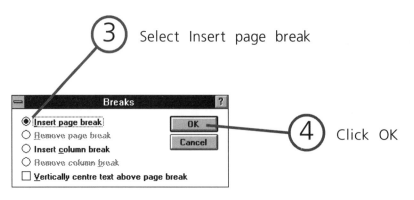

④ Click OK

❑ **To insert a page break**

1 Position the insertion point where you want the page break to occur

2 Open the **Page** menu and choose **Breaks** ....

3 Select **Insert Page Break**

4 Click **OK**

Your insertion point will move to the top of a new page.

Basic steps

☐ **To remove a manual page break**

1 Position the insertion point at the end of the page preceding the page break

2 Open the **Page** menu and choose **Breaks** ....

3 Select **Remove Page Break**

4 Click **OK**

After editing, you may find that your page breaks are no longer in the right places. Removing them is as simple as inserting them.

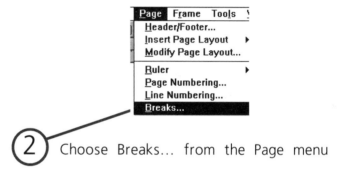

① Place the insertion point at end of page before Page Break

② Choose Breaks... from the Page menu

③ Select Remove page break

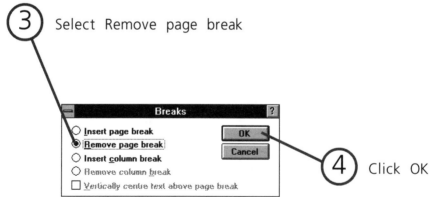

④ Click OK

Turning the pages

If you are working with multi-page documents, there will be times that scrolling through your document using the vertical scroll bar, or using the arrow keys on the keyboard, becomes a bit tedious. There are several ways to make life a bit easier when moving around longer documents, including:-

- Move down to the top of the next page
- Move up to the top of the previous page
- Go to a specific page
- Go to the first page in your document
- Go to the last page in your document

Up Page   Down Page

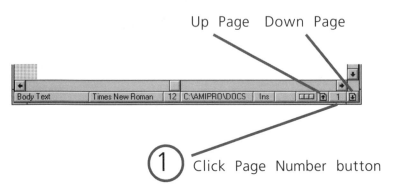

① Click Page Number button

② Choose Page Number

③ Specify Page

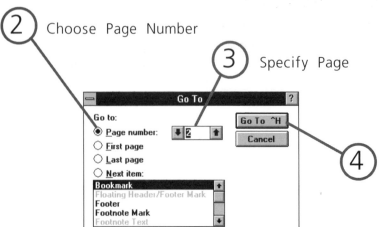

④ Click Go To ^H

❏ **To move up a page**

Click the **UP PAGE** arrow on the status bar

❏ **To move down a page**

Click the **DOWN PAGE** arrow on the status bar

❏ **To go to a specific page**

1 Click the **Page Number** button on the Status Bar

2 Select the **Page Number** option in the **Go To** dialog box

3 Specify the Page Number you want to **Go To**

4 Click the **Go To ^H** button

☐ **To go to the First or Last page**

1 Click the **Page Number** button on the Status Bar

2 Select either the **First page** or **Last page** option in the **Go To** dialog box

3 Click the **Go To ^H** button

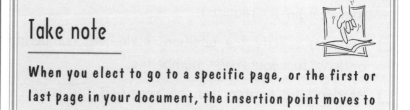

Take note

When you elect to go to a specific page, or the first or last page in your document, the insertion point moves to the **TOP** of the page specified.

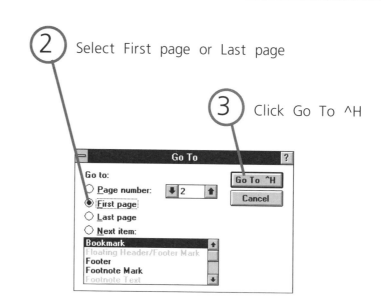

② Select First page or Last page

③ Click Go To ^H

Take note

You must be in Layout Mode to move from page to page as suggested. In Draft Mode you cannot go to a specific page, and the Up page and Down page arrows move you a screen up and screen down respectively.

Summary

- ❏ **Page Numbers** can be placed in the top or bottom margin as required.

- ❏ You can specify the position, style and numbering options for your page numbering.

- ❏ **Headers** and **Footers** can be specified for your document - they will print on every page.

- ❏ To begin a Header or Footer on the second page of your document, choose **Page | Modify Page Layout** and edit the Header or Footer options.

- ❏ Manual **Page Breaks** can be inserted when you want a section of your document to start on a new page.

- ❏ The **Go To** command can help you move through multi-page documents quickly.

11 Columns

Newspaper columns

As an alternative to laying out your text in one column, running from margin to margin, you might want to try newspaper style columns. With newspaper style columns, the text runs from the top to the bottom of the first column, then wraps to the second column and runs from the top to the bottom of the second column and so on until all columns are filled. You can have up to 8 columns in Ami Pro.

1 Click on the **Ruler** to display the **Cols:** field

2 Specify the number of columns required

3 Point and click in the document area (or press [Esc] or [Enter]) to return to your document . The columns set are of equal width.

4 Key in your text. (If you have text already, it is automatically re-arranged into the number of columns specified).

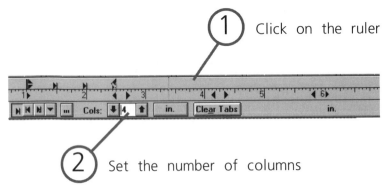

① Click on the ruler

② Set the number of columns

③ Return to the document

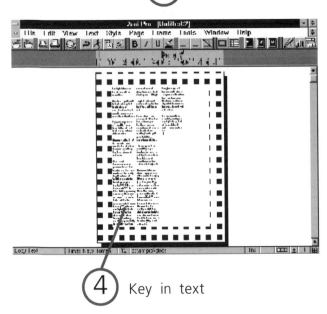

④ Key in text

Take note

Columns are a **Page Layout** feature (like margins). When you set columns using the ruler, the formatting is applied to your whole document.

Basic steps

1 Open the **Page** menu

2 Choose **Modify Page Layout**

3 Check that **Modify Margins & Columns** is selected

4 Specify the **Pages** you want to apply the formatting to

5 Specify the **Number of columns** - the columns will be of equal width

6 Edit the **Gutter width** (the space between the columns) if necessary

7 Click **OK**

Columns in Modify Page Layout

You can also use the Modify Page Layout option in the Page menu to set up columns. If you use Modify Page Layout, you can specify the number of columns for all pages, or for the right or left pages of your document.

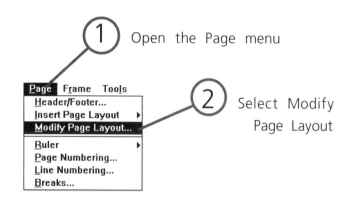

(1) Open the Page menu

(2) Select Modify Page Layout

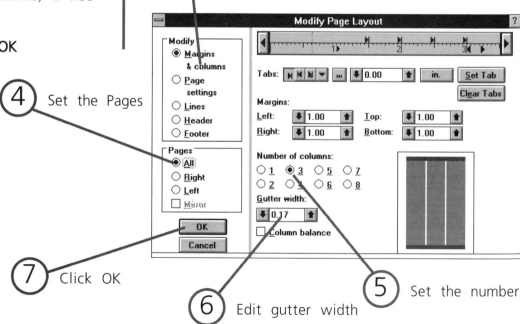

(3) Check that this is selected

(4) Set the Pages

(7) Click OK

(6) Edit gutter width

(5) Set the number

Column & gutter widths

When you set up newspaper style columns, the columns are all of equal width. The gutter margins (the space between each column) are also equal. If you require the columns or the gutters to be of varying widths, you can use the ruler to change them. It does not matter whether the columns were set up using the ruler or the Modify Page Layout dialog box, you must use the ruler to vary the widths.

1   Point, click and drag the **column indent marker** on the ruler to the desired position

❏   Note that you cannot drag the indent marker of one column past the indent marker of another column

2   Point and click in the document area (or press **[Esc]** or **[Enter]**) to return to your document

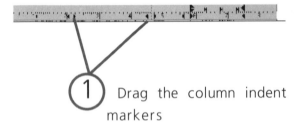

Drag the column indent markers

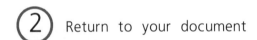

Return to your document

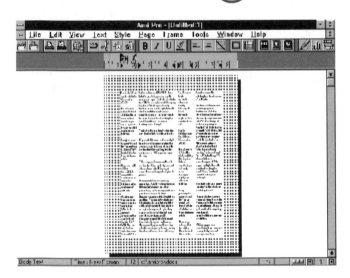

Basic steps

1 Open the **Page** menu
2 Choose **Modify Page Layout**
3 Select the **Modify Lines** option
4 Choose the **Style** of line required
5 Select the **Lines between columns** checkbox
6 Click **OK**

Columns with lines betwen them.

Lines between columns

If you are using newspaper style columns, there are a couple of other features you might want to consider using to enhance the presentation of your work.

The lines between columns option inserts a vertical line between each column. This can clarify the position of each column. There are a variety of line styles you can choose from.

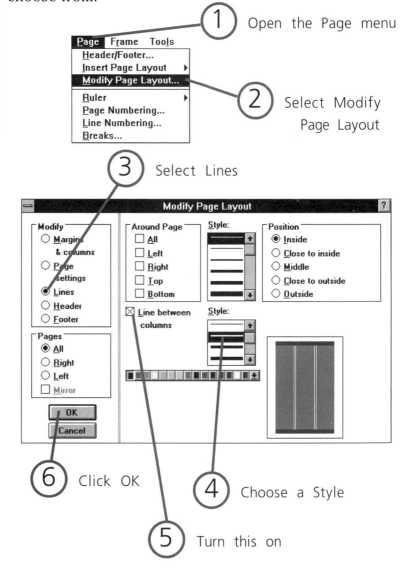

① Open the Page menu

② Select Modify Page Layout

③ Select Lines

⑥ Click OK

④ Choose a Style

⑤ Turn this on

Balancing columns

Column balancing arranges your text in columns of equal length (or as near equal length as possible) - so each column finishes on the same line.

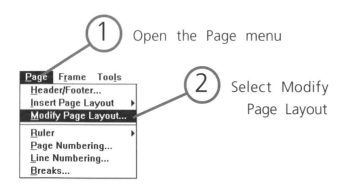

① Open the Page menu

② Select Modify Page Layout

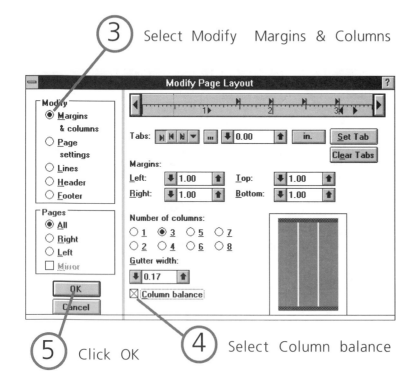

③ Select Modify   Margins & Columns

⑤ Click OK

④ Select Column balance

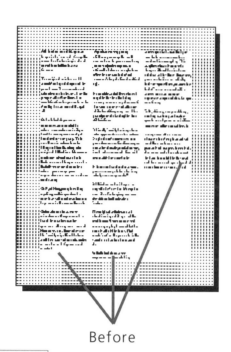

Before

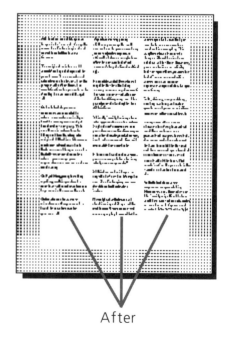

After

Summary

❑ Text can be arranged in several (maximum 8) newspaper style **columns**, rather than in one column running from margin to margin.

❑ Newspaper style columns, and the gutters between them, can be of varying **widths**.

❑ **Column balancing** and vertical **lines** can be used to enhance the appearance of your columns.

12 Frames

Inserting frames

If you need to have different layouts on the same page ie part of a page in a single column and part of a page in several columns, you must use **Frames**.

If you have your document displayed in a number of newspaper style columns, and you want a heading spanning several columns, you use a Frame to contain the heading.

- Frames allow a great deal of versatility in the layout of your documents.

- You can place text or a picture in a Frame.

- Making a frame is very easy.

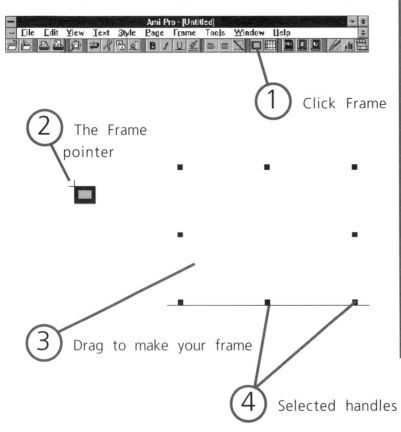

② The Frame pointer

① Click Frame

③ Drag to make your frame

④ Selected handles

1 Click the **Frame** SmartIcon

2 Move the mouse pointer onto the document area - note the Frame mouse pointer

3 Click and drag in the document area to make a Frame - then release the mouse button

4 Note the black handles on each corner and each side of the Frame - the Frame is Selected when you see these handles

❑ To **De-select** a Frame, click anywhere outside it. The handles disappear when it is de-selected.

❑ To **Select** a Frame again, click anywhere inside it. The handles appear again.

Basic steps

Adjusting frames

To resize a Frame

1 Select the Frame

2 Position the mouse pointer over one of the handles - note the double headed arrow pointer

3 Click and drag the handle in the appropriate direction to enlarge or reduce the Frame

To Move a Frame

1 Select the Frame

2 Position the mouse pointer anywhere within the frame

3 Click and drag the frame to the required location

To delete a Frame

1 Select the Frame

2 Press [Delete] on your keyboard

If your frame is too big or too small, you can change its size by clicking and dragging any of its handles.

If it is in the wrong place, you can drag it to where it should be.

If it is no longer required. It can be deleted, without affecting any text that may be inside it.

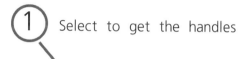

1 Select to get the handles

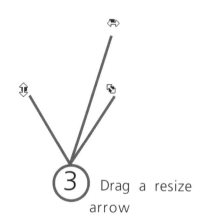

3 Drag a resize arrow

Modifying frame layout

If you want to change the type of Frame, or give your Frame a border, or set tabs or columns within it, you must modify the frame layout.

Basic steps

1 Select the Frame

2 Open the **Frame** menu

3 Choose **Modify Frame Layout**

4 Select the element you want to modify - **Type**, **Size & Position**, **Lines & Shadows** or **Columns & Tabs**

5 Complete the dialog box(es) as required

6 Click **OK** once you have made the necessary modifications

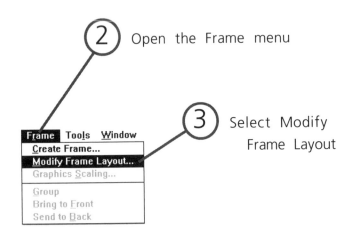

(2) Open the Frame menu

(3) Select Modify Frame Layout

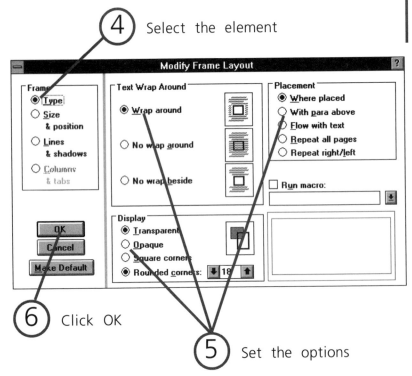

(4) Select the element

(6) Click OK

(5) Set the options

Frame options

Experiment with the Modify Frame Layout dialog box and note how it affects your Frame.

Choosing a Frame option produces a different dialog box. That for Type is shown opposite; the one for Lines is shown below.

Type lets you specify how the other text should wrap around the frame, where the frame should be placed within your document and how the frame should be displayed (transparent or opaque, with square corners or rounded corners).

The **Size & Position** options also include **Margins** fields that let you specify the space between the outside edges of the frame and the text or picture inside it.

In **Lines & Shadows**, you can specify where you want lines (or borders) around your frame. You can choose the line style required, the colour of line and the amount of shadow (if any).

The **Columns & Tabs** option allows you to specify the tabs and columns required *within* your frame.

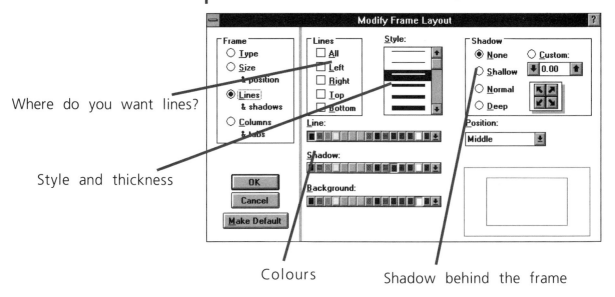

Where do you want lines?

Style and thickness

Colours

Shadow behind the frame

Text within a frame

If you want your text to be displayed in different layouts (ie with different margins or number of columns) on the same page, you must use Frames. You can:-

- Key text into a Frame you have created, or
- Frame existing text

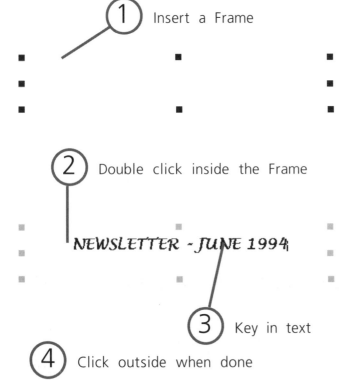

① Insert a Frame

② Double click inside the Frame

NEWSLETTER - JUNE 1994

③ Key in text

④ Click outside when done

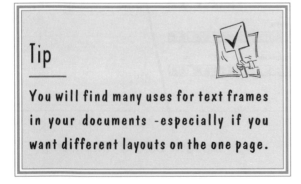

Tip

You will find many uses for text frames in your documents -especially if you want different layouts on the one page.

To key text into a Frame

1 Insert a Frame into your document

2 Double click inside the Frame - the insertion point moves inside the frame and the frame handles become dimmed

3 Key in your text

4 Click anywhere outside the frame when you are finished

❏ If the Frame is the wrong size for the text you have entered, resize it as necessary.

Basic steps

❑ **To Frame existing text**

1 Insert a Frame and drag it around the text. (It will position itself *above* the text)

2 Open the **Frame** menu

3 Choose **Modify Frame Layout**

4 Select the **Type** field in the **Frame** options

5 Select **No wrap around** in the **Text Wrap Around** options

6 Select **Transparent** in the **Display** options

7 Click **OK**

❑ Opposite – framed text spanning three columns

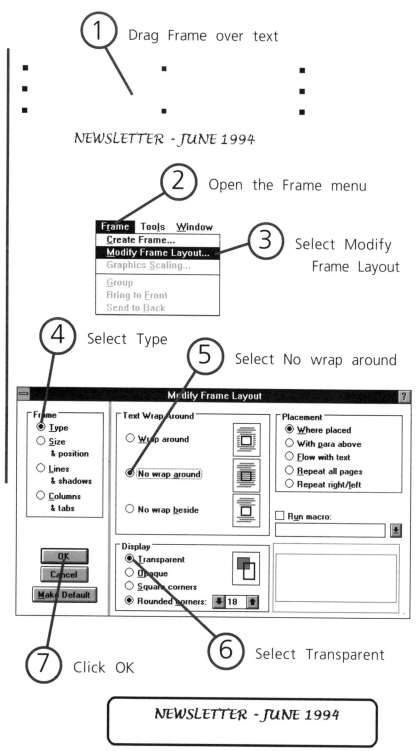

① Drag Frame over text

NEWSLETTER - JUNE 1994

② Open the Frame menu

③ Select Modify Frame Layout

④ Select Type

⑤ Select No wrap around

⑥ Select Transparent

⑦ Click OK

NEWSLETTER - JUNE 1994

Using AmiDraw graphics

There may be times when you feel like livening your documents up a bit by including some graphics (pictures). You do not need to be able to draw the graphics yourself, as Ami Pro comes with 105 graphic images ready for you to use. The supplied images cover a range of themes - computers, music, office, education, travel - try them out, you might find something useful!

There are 2 stages to including a graphic:-

● Make a Frame for you picture

● Import your picture

Make a Frame as shown on page 114.

Make a Frame as shown on page 114.

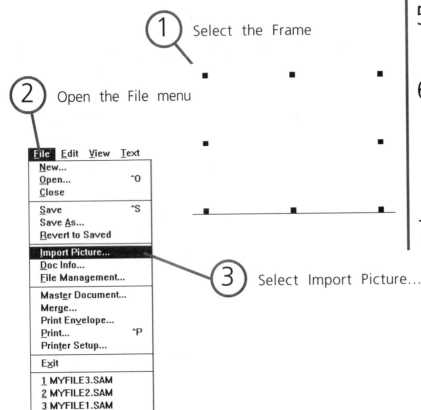

① Select the Frame

② Open the File menu

③ Select Import Picture...

File menu:
- New...
- Open...   ^O
- Close
- Save   ^S
- Save As...
- Revert to Saved
- **Import Picture...**
- Doc Info...
- File Management...
- Master Document...
- Merge...
- Print Envelope...
- Print...   ^P
- Printer Setup...
- Exit
- 1 MYFILE3.SAM
- 2 MYFILE2.SAM
- 3 MYFILE1.SAM
- 4 OLDNAME.SAM

Basic steps

1 Select the Frame into which you wish to Import your picture (if you have de-selected the frame, point and click anywhere within it to select it again).

2 Open the **File** menu

3 Select **Import Picture** ...

4 Select **AmiDraw** in the **File type** list

5 Select the Picture file from the list displayed

6 Select the **Copy Image** checkbox if necessary - this ensures a *copy* of the picture is imported and not the original

7 Click **OK**

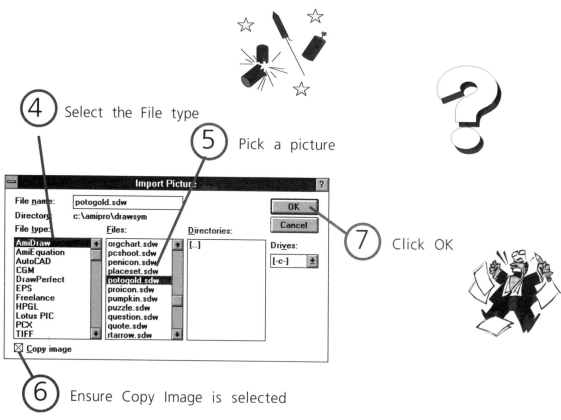

④ Select the File type

⑤ Pick a picture

Import Picture

File name: potogold.sdw

Directory: c:\amipro\drawsym

File type:
- AmiDraw
- AmiEquation
- AutoCAD
- CGM
- DrawPerfect
- EPS
- Freelance
- HPGL
- Lotus PIC
- PCX
- TIFF

Files:
- orgchart.sdw
- pcshoot.sdw
- penicon.sdw
- placeset.sdw
- potogold.sdw
- proicon.sdw
- pumpkin.sdw
- puzzle.sdw
- question.sdw
- quote.sdw
- rtarrow.sdw

Directories:
[..]

Drives:
[-c-]

OK

Cancel

⑦ Click OK

☒ Copy image

⑥ Ensure Copy Image is selected

Tip

Combining your skills using columns, frames and importing pictures, you can produce interesting displays and documents using Ami Pro.

Summary

❑ Frames can contain **text** or **pictures**.

❑ Frames can be used to give **different layouts** on a single page.

❑ Frames can be resized, moved or deleted easily.

❑ There are a set of **sdw** graphic files, supplied with AmiPro, which can liven up your documents.

❑ AmiPro can also **Import Pictures** from other graphics packages.

13 File management

Changing directories

Basic steps

File Management is essential to keep your data safe, up-to-date and well organised. When you need to format diskettes or organise your directory structure, you must go into File Manager in Windows itself. From within Ami Pro, however, you can manage your files by:-

● Copying

● Moving

● Renaming

● Deleting

We'll consider each of these in the next few pages.

1 Open the **File** menu

2 Choose **File Man-agement** ...

the Current Directory file list is displayed

❏ **To view a different drive and/or directory**

3 Open the **File** menu in the File Manager window and choose **Change Directory**

4 Key in the drive/directory path you want to view

5 Click **OK**

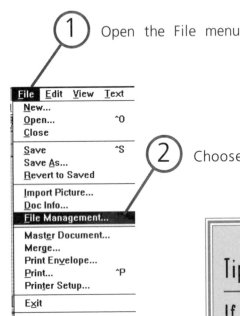

① Open the File menu

File	Edit	View	Text
New...			
Open...		^O	
Close			
Save		^S	
Save As...			
Revert to Saved			
Import Picture...			
Doc Info...			
File Management...			
Master Document...			
Merge...			
Print Envelope...			
Print...		^P	
Printer Setup...			
Exit			

② Choose File Management..

Tip

If the drive/directory you want to view is displayed on the list, you can view it by double clicking on it

❏ You can copy, move, rename or delete files displayed in the list, using the commands on the File menu

Current directory

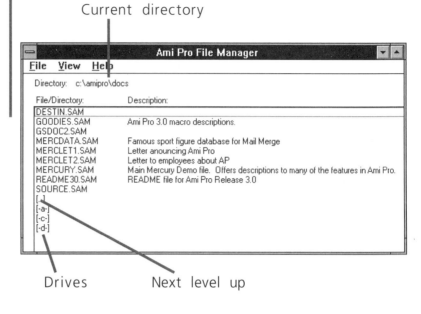

Drives   Next level up

③ Choose Change Directory.. from the new File menu

⑤ Click OK

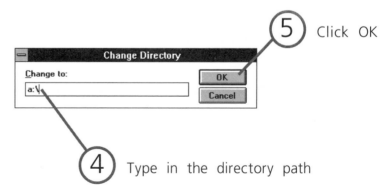

④ Type in the directory path

Finding files

When you go into File Management, the files listed are Ami Pro files (with a .S?M extension). If you want to view files that are not Ami Pro files, or only specific files, you can use the **View** menu to specify the files you want.

- ❑ **To list ALL file types**
- 1 Open the **View** menu and choose **All**
- ❑ **To list specific types of files**
- 1 Open the **View** menu and choose **Partial...**
- 2 Key in the enough detail to specify the files you want to view, using Wildcard characters as necessary
- 3 Click **OK**

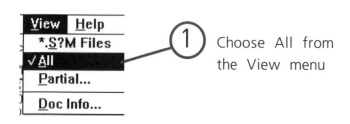

Choose All from the View menu

Choose Partial.. from the View menu

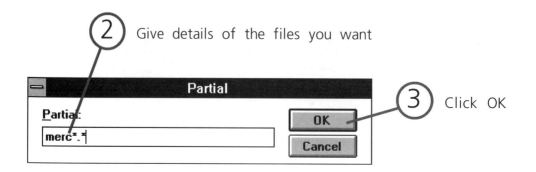

Give details of the files you want

Click OK

Wildcard characters

When specifying filenames and/or extensions you can use **?** to represent any single character that might vary, or ***** to represent a string of characters that might vary.

*.DOC would find and display filenames like **report.doc, ms2.doc, memo.doc**

AA*.* would find and display filenames like **AAletter.clp, AAmemo.doc, AAlist.sam**

CHAPTER?.SAM would find and display filenames like **chapter1.sam, chapter2.sam, chapter3.sam**

The files list from **merc*.***

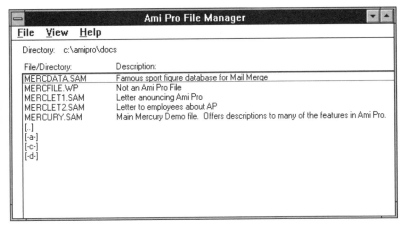

1 2 7

Copying files

It is essential to copy files for security reasons. If you do not have a copy of a file, and your disk gets damaged, you might end up losing your file - undesirable if it is several pages long and took some time to generate!

You can copy a file to:-

● a different drive

● a different directory

● a new file on the same drive/directory, provided you specify a filename that is different from the original one

You can copy one or more files at a time.

1 Open the **File** menu

2 Choose **File Management**

3 Display the directory that contains the file you want to copy

4 Point and click to select the file (or files) to be copied - if you select the wrong one, deselect it by clicking on it again

5 Open the **File** menu and choose **Copy**

6 Complete the **Copy** dialog box to specify where the files are to be copied to

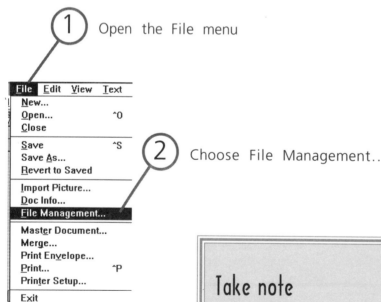

Open the File menu

Choose File Management..

File	Edit	View	Text
New...			
Open...		^O	
Close			
Save		^S	
Save As...			
Revert to Saved			
Import Picture...			
Doc Info...			
File Management...			
Master Document...			
Merge...			
Print Envelope...			
Print...		^P	
Printer Setup...			
Exit			

Take note

If you are copying a file onto the same drive and directory as the original, you must give it a different filename - at step 6 above, specify the **path** and **filename** to copy the file to, e.g. **C:\AMIPRO\DOCS\FILENAME.SAM**

7 Click **OK**

8 At the **File Copy Options** dialog box, click **OK** again.

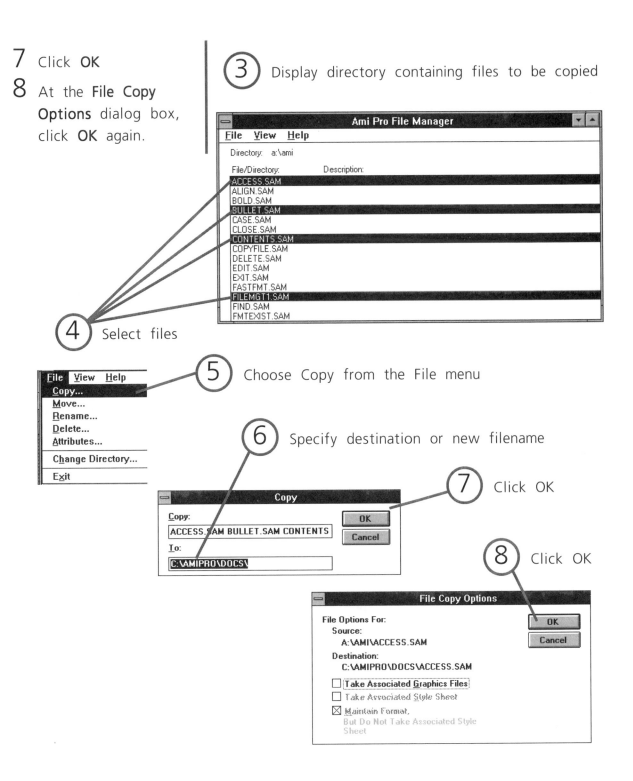

③ Display directory containing files to be copied

Ami Pro File Manager

File   View   Help

Directory: a:\ami

File/Directory: Description:

ACCESS.SAM
ALIGN.SAM
BOLD.SAM
BULLET.SAM
CASE.SAM
CLOSE.SAM
CONTENTS.SAM
COPYFILE.SAM
DELETE.SAM
EDIT.SAM
EXIT.SAM
FASTFMT.SAM
FILEMGT1.SAM
FIND.SAM
FMTEXIST.SAM

④ Select files

File   View   Help
Copy...
Move...
Rename...
Delete...
Attributes...
Change Directory...
Exit

⑤ Choose Copy from the File menu

⑥ Specify destination or new filename

Copy

Copy:
ACCESS.SAM BULLET.SAM CONTENTS

To:
C:\AMIPRO\DOCS\

OK
Cancel

⑦ Click OK

⑧ Click OK

File Copy Options

File Options For:
Source:
A:\AMI\ACCESS.SAM
Destination:
C:\AMIPRO\DOCS\ACCESS.SAM

☐ Take Associated Graphics Files
☐ Take Associated Style Sheet
☒ Maintain Format,
But Do Not Take Associated Style Sheet

OK
Cancel

129

Moving files

There may be times when you decide your file is in the wrong place! It may be on the wrong disk, or in the wrong directory. You can easily move your file to a new location.

You can move a file to a different:-

● drive

● directory

You can move one or more files at a time, as long as they are all going to the same destination.

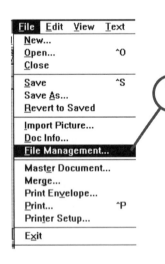

Choose File Management.. from the File menu

1 Open the **File** menu and choose **File Management**

2 Display the directory that contains the file you want to move

3 Point and click to select the file (or files) to be moved - point and click on them again to deselect a wrong choice

4 Open the **File** menu and choose **Move**

5 Complete the **Move** dialog box to specify where the files are to be moved to

Take note

When moving a single file, you can specify a new filename for the destination file if required - at step **5** above, specify the **path** and **filename** to move the file to ie A:\NEWNAME.SAM

6 Click **OK**

7 At the **File Move Options** dialog box, click **OK** again

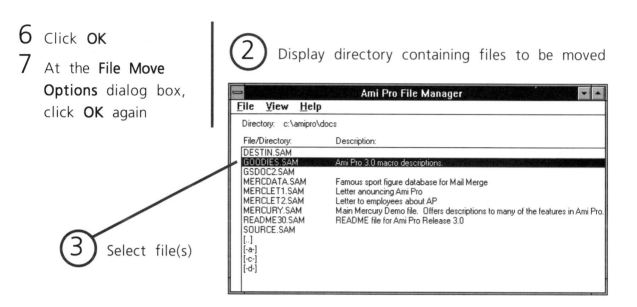

② Display directory containing files to be moved

③ Select file(s)

④ Choose Move from the File menu

⑤ Specify destination or new filename

⑥ Click OK

⑦ Click OK

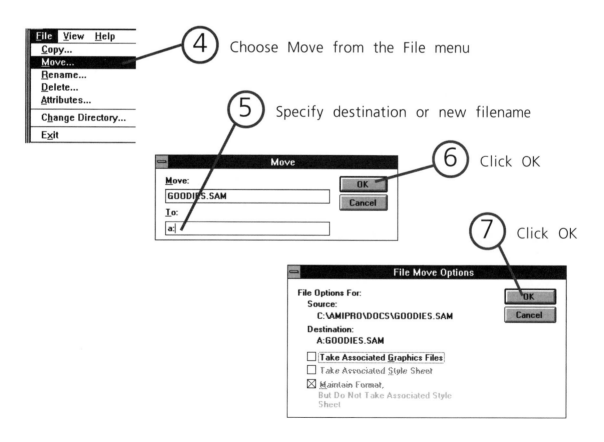

Renaming files

If you get to the stage where you have got the right file, in the right place, but with the wrong name, you can rename it to something more suitable.

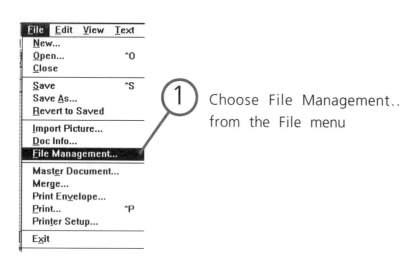

Choose File Management.. from the File menu

1 Open the **File** menu and choose **File Management**

2 Display the directory that contains the file you want to rename

3 Select the file to be renamed - just point and click on it

4 Open the **File** menu and choose **Rename**

5 Complete the **Rename** dialog box to specify the new name for the file

6 Click **OK**

7 Note the new filename

② Display directory containing files to be renamed

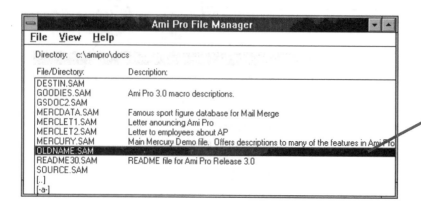

③ Select files

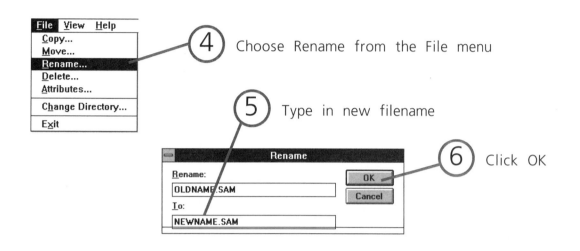

④ Choose Rename from the File menu

⑤ Type in new filename

⑥ Click OK

⑦ New filename

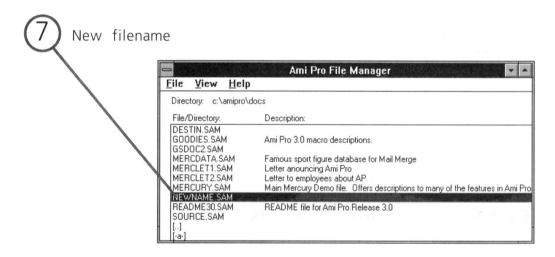

Deleting files

The time will come when you decide it is time to tidy up your directories a bit and delete some data files that you no longer need. If you keep everything you ever produce, you will end up running out of disk space - unless you have a very big disk.

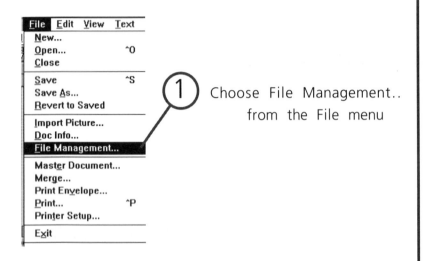

Choose File Management.. from the File menu

Basic steps

1 Open the **File** menu and choose **File Management**

2 Display the directory that contains the file you want to delete

3 Point and click to select the file (or files) to be deleted - if you select the wrong one, you can deselect it by clicking on it again

4 Open the **File** menu and choose **Delete...**

5 Confirm the deletion by clicking **OK** at the **Delete** dialog box (or **Cancel**, if you've changed your mind)

Display directory containing files to be deleted

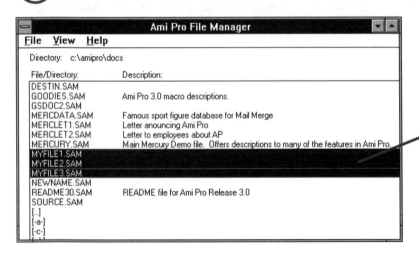

Select files

1 3 4

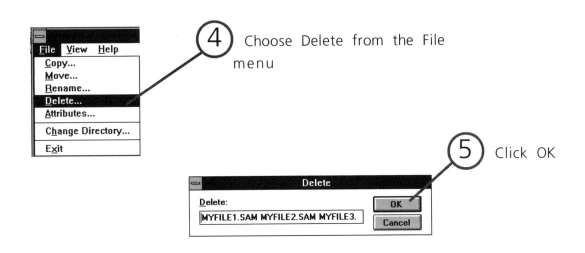

④ Choose Delete from the File menu

⑤ Click OK

Files deleted

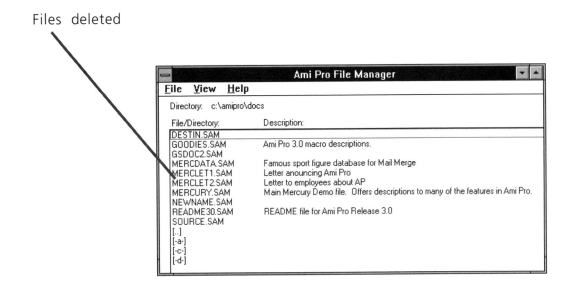

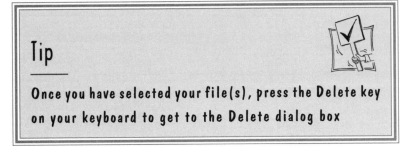

Tip

Once you have selected your file(s), press the Delete key on your keyboard to get to the Delete dialog box

Summary

❏ **File Management** can be performed from within Ami Pro (without going out into File Manager in Windows)

❏ Files can be **Copied**, **Moved**, **Renamed** or **Deleted** using the menu sequence:

   File | File Management | File command

14 Document information

Recording details

You may find that the maximum 8 character file name limitation can lead to some pretty cryptic file names at times. If (or when) this is the case, you can complete the **Document Description** field in the **Save As** dialog box to explain the contents of your file in greater detail.

If you need to record additional information to explain what is in your file, or give details of the author, operator, recipient - indeed any information you consider relevant - you could use the **Document Information** feature.

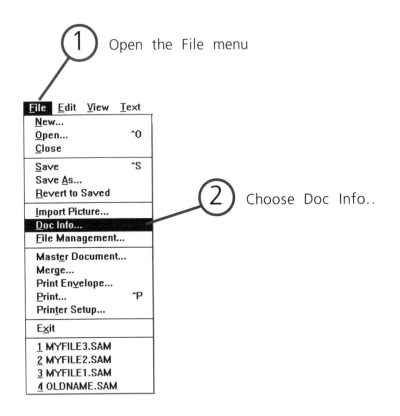

Open the File menu

Choose Doc Info..

1 Open the **File** menu

2 Choose **Doc Info** ...

3 Complete the **Description** field as you wish (this field also appears in the **Save As** and **Open** dialog boxes)

4 Complete the **Keywords** field with any keywords you consider appropriate

5 Click **OK** to return to your document

Tip

You can print out the Document Information details as a cover sheet for your document. To do so, choose **Options**, from the **Print** dialog box and select the **With Document Description** checkbox.

Let's say you have created a document on weekend breaks in the Borders. The file has been called *weborder*. You can use the Description and/or Keyword fields to describe the file. Use the **Description** field to give a fuller explanation of the file's contents. For example, "Weekend breaks in the Scottish Borders, full and half board accommodation, Summer 1994."

In the **Keywords** field you can give other details that you consider to be important about the file, such as, the towns mentioned in your document, i.e. "Kelso, Melrose".

③ Give document description details

⑤ Click OK

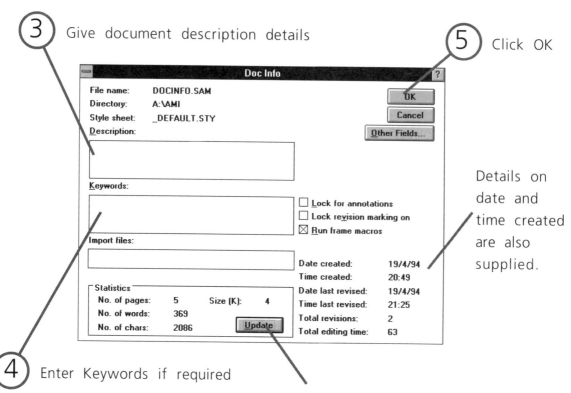

Details on date and time created are also supplied.

④ Enter Keywords if required

Note the additional statistical information supplied about your document - the statistics can be brought up to date by clicking **Update**.

Using other fields

If you want to record additional details about the document, there is a set of **Other Fields** for this purpose.

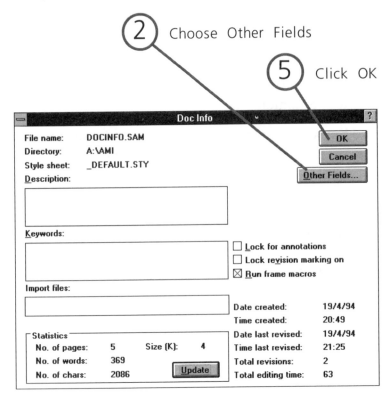

② Choose Other Fields

⑤ Click OK

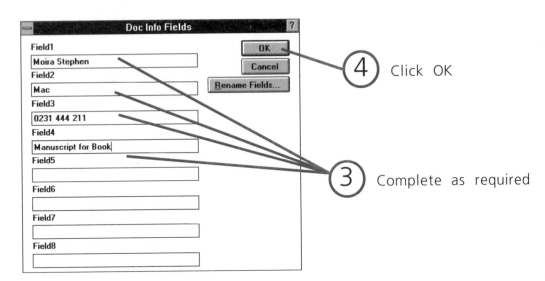

④ Click OK

③ Complete as required

1 4 0

Basic steps

1 Display the **Other Fields...** dialog box (see steps 1-2 above)

2 Choose **Rename Fields..**

3 Rename the fields to suit your needs (press [Tab] or [Shift]-[Tab] to move forward or backwards through the fields)

4 Click **OK** to return to the **Other Fields** dialog box

5 Click **OK** to return to the **Doc Info** dialog box

Renaming fields

If you find the field names in the **Other Fields** dialog box unsuitable, (Field1, Field2, Field3 etc are not the most meaningful field names to use!) you can easily rename them to suit your document(s).

④ Click OK

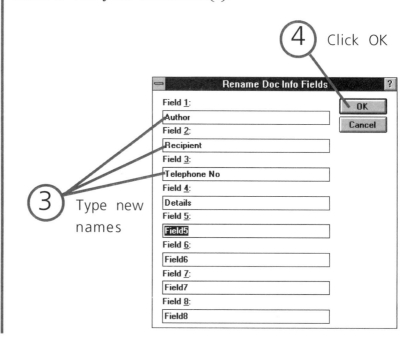

③ Type new names

⑤ Click OK

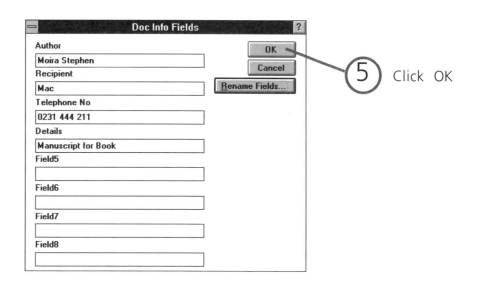

Inserting Doc Info fields

The fields you complete in the Doc Info... dialog box can be inserted into your document if desired. This can be very useful for reference purposes - incorporating a filename and/or path into a reference, header or footer can make it easy to locate files on disk when you are looking at the hardcopy.

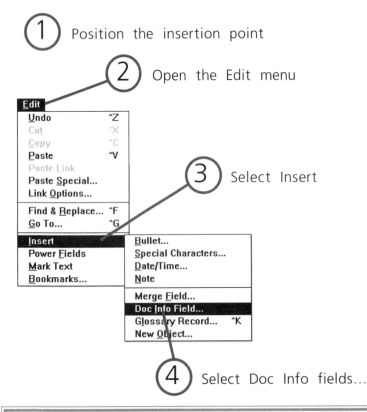

Position the insertion point

Open the Edit menu

Select Insert

Select Doc Info fields...

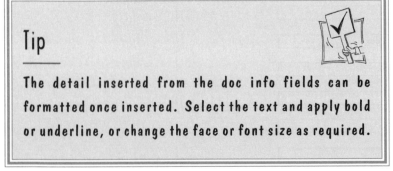

Tip

The detail inserted from the doc info fields can be formatted once inserted. Select the text and apply bold or underline, or change the face or font size as required.

7 When you have inserted all the Doc Info Fields required, click **Cancel** to close the dialog box.

❑ If you decide to delete the detail inserted from a Doc Info Field, simply select the text and press **[Delete]**.

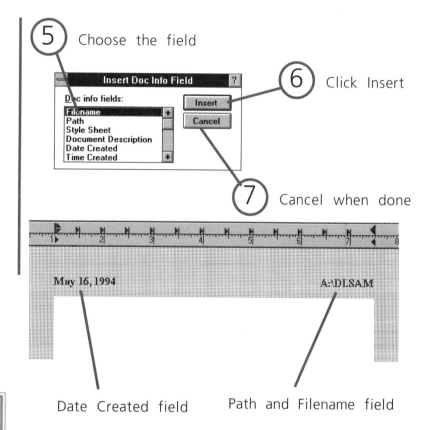

⑤ Choose the field

⑥ Click Insert

⑦ Cancel when done

Date Created field   Path and Filename field

all inserted into Header area

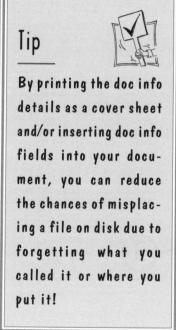

Tip

By printing the doc info details as a cover sheet and/or inserting doc info fields into your document, you can reduce the chances of misplacing a file on disk due to forgetting what you called it or where you put it!

143

Identifying files

When carrying out File Management activities, you can view the Document Info screen for any selected file before deleting, copying etc to help establish you have the correct one.

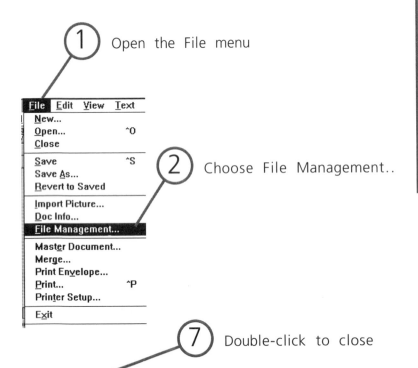

Open the File menu

Choose File Management..

Double-click to close

File Edit View Text
New...
Open...   ^O
Close
Save   ^S
Save As...
Revert to Saved
Import Picture...
Doc Info...
File Management...
Master Document...
Merge...
Print Envelope...
Print...   ^P
Printer Setup...
Exit

Ami Pro File Manager

File   View   Help

Directory: c:\amipro\docs

File/Directory:	Description:
DESTIN.SAM	
GOODIES.SAM	Ami Pro 3.0 macro descriptions.
GSDOC2.SAM	
MERCDATA.SAM	Famous sport figure database for Mail Merge
MERCLET1.SAM	Letter anouncing Ami Pro
MERCLET2.SAM	Letter to employees about AP
MERCURY.SAM	Main Mercury Demo file. Offers descriptions to many of the features in Ami Pro
OLDNAME.SAM	
README30.SAM	README file for Ami Pro Release 3.0
SOURCE.SAM	
[..]	
[-a-]	

Select your file

Basic steps

1 Open the **File** menu

2 Choose **File Management**

3 Select the file you want to delete/copy/move/rename

4 Open the **View** menu

5 Choose **Doc Info...**

☐ The Document Information screen for the selected document is displayed.

❏ When you are finished with the dialog box:

6 Click **OK** to return to the **File Management** dialog box.

7 Double click the control box in the **File Management** dialog box to return to your document when ready.

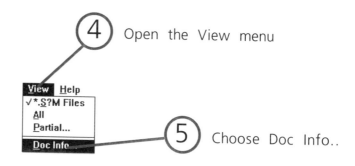

④ Open the View menu

View Help
√*.S?M Files
All
Partial...
Doc Info

⑤ Choose Doc Info..

⑥ Click OK to return to the File Management box

Doc Info

File name: **MERCLET1.SAM**
Directory: **c:\amipro\docs**
Style sheet: **None**
Description:
Letter anouncing Ami Pro

[**OK**]
[**Cancel**]
[**Other Fields...**]

☐ Lock for annotations
☒ Run frame macros

Keywords:

Import files:

┌ Statistics ──────────
  No. of pages: 2   Size (K):   0
  No. of words: 0
  No. of chars: 0

Date created: 1/6/92
Time created: 11:46
Date last rev: 28/7/92
Total revisions: 9
Total editing time: 6

Summary

❑ **Document Information** can be used to record additional details about your document.

❑ As well as the Description, Keywords, Statistics and Date details on the main dialog box, there are **Other Fields** that can be used to record extra items.

❑ In **File Management**, you can access the Document Information screen on any document you intend to copy, move, rename or delete. This is useful if you are in any doubt that you have the correct document.

Index